The Feminine Eye

RECOGNITIONS

detective/suspense

Bruce Cassiday, General Editor

Raymond Chandler by Jerry Speir
P. D. James by Norma Siebenheller
John D. MacDonald by David Geherin
Ross MacDonald by Jerry Speir
Dorothy L. Sayers by Dawson Gaillard
Sons of Sam Spade: The Private Eye Novel in the 70s
by David Geherin

science fiction

Tom Staicar, General Editor

Isaac Asimov by Jean Fiedler and Jim Mele
Ray Bradbury by Wayne L. Johnson
Critical Encounters: Writers and Themes in Science Fiction, edited
by Dick Riley
Critical Encounters II: Writers and Themes in Science Fiction,
edited by Tom Staicar
The Feminine Eye: Science Fiction and the Women Who Write It,
edited by Tom Staicar
Frank Herbert by Timothy O'Reilly
Ursula K. LeGuin by Barbara J. Bucknall
Theodore Sturgeon by Lucy Menger

Also of Interest

The Bedside, Bathtub & Armchair Companion to Agatha Christie,
edited by Dick Riley and Pam McAllister
Introduction by Julian Symons

THE FEMININE EYE

Science Fiction and the Women Who Write It

Edited by Tom Staicar

FREDERICK UNGAR PUBLISHING CO.   NEW YORK

Copyright © 1982 by Frederick Ungar Publishing Co., Inc.
Printed in the United States of America

Library of Congress Cataloging in Publication Data

Main entry under title:

The Feminine eye.
  (Recognitions)
  Bibliography: p.
  Contents: Leigh Brackett: no long goodbye is good enough / Rosemarie
Arbur — C. L. Moore's classic science fiction / Patricia Mathews — Andre
Norton: humanity amid the hardware / Roger C. Schlobin — [etc.]
  1. Science fiction, American—Women authors—History and
criticism. 2. American fiction—20th century—History and
criticism. 3. Feminism and literature. 4. Sex role in
literature. I. Staicar, Tom.
II. Series.
PS347.S35F45   813'.0876'099287   81-70120
ISBN 0-8044-2838-7   AACR2
ISBN 0-8044-6878-8 (pbk.)

Contents

Editor's Foreword

This book deals with one of the most important aspects of modern science fiction: the writings of some of the women who have chosen SF as a vehicle for their views. The essays can be read with pleasure and understanding by newcomers to the field, by the lifelong SF fan, and by students in women's studies courses. All the essays are based on solid research. Written by experts but aimed at the nonspecialist, they explore the sex roles and attitudes prevalent in societies of the future, in which women and men live their lives in ways found nowhere on Earth today.

Science fiction has lured a number of new writers from the feminist movement partly because only SF permits unlimited freedom in the settings and situations of feminist fiction. Mainstream novels restrict their writers either to a historical setting where sex roles are already established, or to contemporary settings where potential future sex roles do not exist except for isolated individuals. Only science fiction allows the freedom to create a "laboratory" world where one can experiment with matriarchal societies that dominate entire nations, group marriages, radical approaches to child rearing, and other feminist speculations about alternatives to existing sex roles and living arrangements.

Women have always written SF, whether in the days of Mary Wollstonecraft Shelley's *Frankenstein*, the early pulp magazine era, or the current period. In the minority both in the reading audience and the contents pages of the SF magazines until the 1970s, women now constitute a major portion of both. In several recent ballotings for Hugo and Nebula awards, women outnumbered men. Such names as Le Guin, McIntyre, Tiptree, and Vinge are listed among the winners of those awards as well as the World Fantasy Awards and others.

The Feminine Eye deals with some of the most impressive writers and their themes:

What if the roles of men and women were reversed in a future society, with men taking a relatively passive role while women took the important positions in business, government, the professions and the military? Carolyn J. Cherryh explores the consequences of this type of world in her novels, examined in a thought-provoking essay.

The price to be paid for freedom is one of the themes of Marion Zimmer Bradley's famous Darkover novels.

The Nebula Award for Best Novel in 1980 was won by Suzy McKee Charnas for *The Vampire Tapestry*, subject of an essay that sets her story of modern vampirism into perspective for the reader.

"James Tiptree, Jr." created a sensation in the SF world in the mid-1970s and became known as a man who understood the feminist viewpoint. "Tiptree" was revealed to be a pseudonym of feminist writer Alice Sheldon, a woman of mature years who decided to use a man's name.

Andre Norton, Catherine L. Moore, and Leigh Brackett each broke into the SF field at a time when women were not welcomed by the young males who made up a majority of the pre-1960s SF readership. Each went on to succeed as popular and critical acclaim rewarded their efforts.

These are some of the topics in *The Feminine Eye*. Although this collection does not, of course, discuss the work of all women who have written SF, this is a constraint of space rather than a critical judgment. Along with the essays, all written especially for this volume, there are notes at the end of the book and suggestions for further reading.

We hope *The Feminine Eye* will both entertain you and show you new aspects of the significant contributions of women to science fiction.

T. S.

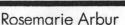

Rosemarie Arbur

LEIGH BRACKETT: No "Long Goodbye" Is Good Enough

On March 18, 1978, in a hospital not very far from the place of her birth, Leigh Brackett died. While it can be said of many persons that they died too soon, the cliché, from the perspective of those who love science fiction and the many worlds it has created, is particularly appropriate for Brackett. Books such as the one you are reading had only begun to be published in the mid-seventies, and by 1976 Leigh Brackett, sixty-three at her death in 1978, had published all but two of her hundred works of fiction. Her death consigned her to the past before her work could be adequately discussed in the present. Thus, for most readers of science fiction—especially those who like also to read *about* science fiction—Brackett has been relegated to the status of a historical figure. A lively one, it should be said—her last achievement was the screenplay for the sequel to *Star Wars*: the immensely popular *The Empire Strikes Back*.

With few exceptions, Brackett's works have not been presented seriously to those too young ever to have read the pulps, to those too old to consider science fiction equal in value to the other, more traditional forms of literature, and to those who regard science fiction as the chief literary movement of this century. Brackett's achievements only rarely find themselves in the company of those that deserve (if not demand) respectful critical scrutiny as well as hours of enjoyable reading.

But they do belong in that company. Because they do, I take my title from a major screenplay she wrote and turn its emphasis around: the objective of this essay is not to look *back* at Leigh Brackett's science fiction accomplishments as if they were receding toward a region inaccessible to us because it no longer exists; the objective is to look at them straight on, as they (still) really are. If readers of this essay are somehow influenced to look into what they have not already read or to reread a favorite Brackett tale, or to examine and adjust the list of authors in their secret, personal SF hall of fame, then this essay—the French word is "attempt"—will have succeeded. In the excitement of (re)discovering the fine things Brackett did with language, readers may forget the need to say their goodbyes, for they will have immersed themselves in prose that is strong, timeless, and alive.

The only child of William Franklin Brackett and Margaret Douglass Brackett, Leigh Douglass Brackett was born in Los Angeles on December 7, 1915. She was educated in private, all-girls' schools—her teachers were Catholic nuns—where she developed her life-long love of literature and drama. We may assume that her teachers not only imparted a strict, no-nonsense approach to the proprieties of written English but also stood as role models—dedicated professionals and figures of authority, almost all women. These assumptions and the facts from which they are inferred become important to an understanding of the kind of feminine characters we find in Brackett's science fiction. Of equal relevance is the practical necessity in an all-girls' school for students of drama to concentrate on the characters—not the characters' gender—in the plays they perform. Thus, although not unusual, it is nonetheless significant that when Brackett starred in her senior play, her role was that of a masculine character.

Outside of school, Brackett read and reread the works of Edgar Rice Burroughs. She also spent her summers at her grandparents' home on the beach, where she also made some important contacts. By 1939 Brackett had become a member of the science fiction world, since, on Sundays, after she played volleyball on Muscle Beach, Ray Bradbury would meet her with his works-in-progress for her to read and discuss. She was befriended by Henry Kuttner who, Bradbury recalls, "was one of our teachers. . . . [He] told us about Katherine Anne Porter and Eudora Welty and Raymond Chandler and [other writers] with very clean styles." Another such teacher and friend was Edmond Hamilton, already a successful science fiction writer, whom Brackett eventually married. Half-seriously, Hamilton has said that the "yes" to his proposal was the result of Forrest J. Ackerman's literary matchmaking: Brackett had repeatedly mentioned her desire to read E. R. Eddison's

The Worm Ouroboros, an exceedingly difficult book to locate. When Hamilton was able to lend her a copy, which he had borrowed from Ackerman's even-then-tremendous private collection, Brackett was so delighted that she agreed to marry him.

That Brackett and Bradbury had "writing workshops" on the beach is, for persons well acquainted with both authors, almost common knowledge; the other anecdotal information is not. It is genuinely "new" background material and, equally important, it emphasizes the literary—not just science fictional—orientation of these writers. According to Bradbury (careful reading of Brackett's science fiction confirms this), Brackett was a true "student of writing." Like her friends, she was seriously interested in contemporary (and traditional) "mainstream literature" for its own sake, but she was especially appreciative of its artistry and was eager to incorporate its best attributes in her own fiction. Because it has taken so long for science fiction to get academic recognition, it is still, Bradbury says, "little known that science fiction writers care about literature."

In fact, most of them care enough to risk general unpopularity in order to produce a literature that is truly contemporary, a literature that addresses the real concerns of a culture that is racing into the future. It is important to know that Brackett was conscious that her science fiction was a contribution to this culturally avant-garde literature. It is also important to know that she could and did write commercially successful and highly regarded screenplays, teleplays, "tough" detective novels, and even a western that earned a best-of-the-year award. What is downright awesome is that Brackett was "pretty much a first-draft writer." That is, the science fiction tales we read and praise for their stylistic strength and beauty are often, almost word for word, the narratives as they existed after she put the final period in place. That such a writer became the "undisputed Queen of Space Opera" is hardly surprising.

Were it not for Brackett's versatility, however, it would surprise some that her first two published stories—"Martian Quest" and "The Treasure of Ptakuth"—met the rigorous technical standards of magazine editor John W. Campbell. They appeared in the 1940 February and April issues of *Astounding* (which later became *Analog*) and officially began Brackett's professional science fiction career. In 1944 her first novel—*No Good from a Corpse*—was published; its dialogue was so realistic that Howard Hawks sought her out to collaborate with William

Faulkner on the screenplay for *The Big Sleep* the very same year. Thus, after the publication of at least twenty-two stories in science fiction magazines, Brackett won acclaim with a novel-length mystery. Then, after four more science fiction tales in print and about ten thousand words of "Lorelei of the Red Mist" in typescript (which she gave to Ray Bradbury to finish), she found herself coauthor of a film in which Humphrey Bogart starred.

Another cliché is in order: "That was only the beginning." On January 1, 1947 she and Edmond Hamilton entered into a marriage that lasted until his death more than thirty years later. By 1950 their efforts at rebuilding the old farmhouse in Kinsman, Ohio, near Hamilton's home town, were rewarded by its being comfortable enough to live in; thereafter they spent summers in Lancaster (near Los Angeles) and returned to Kinsman each fall. Brackett continued to write scripts for Hollywood as well as stories and novelettes for *Planet Stories, Thrilling Wonder Stories*, and similar pulp magazines. She began her work with longer science fiction forms first by expanding previously published works (the evolution of *The Sword of Rhiannon* is particularly fascinating) and later, as *The Long Tomorrow* (1955) demonstrates, by conscious planning of a preconceived novel. With the publication of *The Book of Skaith* in 1976, it became clear that she had mastered the art of the trilogy and, incidentally, that she had produced one of the very best middle books (*The Hounds of Skaith*, 1974) yet to appear as part of the three-volume form.

While her collaboration with Ray Bradbury—"Lorelei of the Red Mist," 1946—is more accurately a serial coauthorship (Brackett began the story, stopped, and Bradbury took it on through its conclusion; neither altered a single word the other had written), Brackett's and Hamilton's "Stark and the Star Kings" is a true joint effort. It is as well the only work that she and her husband wrote together and the catalyst that led Brackett to expand her science fiction settings beyond our solar system.

The genesis of the ten-thousand-word story is both interesting and revelatory. Harlan Ellison, who had known the couple since 1950 or 1951, asked them to contribute to his *The Last Dangerous Visions* by writing a single story about their all-time favorite characters. In response, Brackett and Hamilton not only broke a thirty-year-old habit of keeping to their own typewriters but set aside the general rule they seem tacitly to have agreed upon: that Brackett wrote interplanetary and Hamilton interstellar adventures. "Stark and the Star Kings" was completed during the summer of 1973. For the authors it was an exciting, liberating, and immensely enjoyable story to write, and for Ellison it is a tangible yet priceless expression of their reciprocated influence and love.

In 1977 *The Best of Edmond Hamilton* appeared; it was a collection of stories selected, edited, and introduced by Brackett. During the same year Hamilton died; Brackett turned (or returned) to writing her fourth set-on-Skaith novel. Then she put aside her unfinished novel to accept George Lucas's request that she write the script for the sequel to *Star Wars*, *The Empire Strikes Back*. She transformed Lucas's story into a screenplay (also inventing the Snowbeast), writing until she had completed a full first draft. Shortly thereafter, she died.

In its most accurate sense, "Queen of Space Opera" denotes Leigh Brackett's special kind of personal eminence far more than its suggests any artificial regality. She won only one award—the Jules Verne Award for "The Last Days of Shandakor"—for a work of science fiction, yet her readers and her friends loved her. After three decades in the science fiction world, Harlan Ellison thought "she [was] one of the finest people I have ever known." Jack Williamson, whose acquaintance with Brackett goes back about forty years, agrees that her prose is among the finest to be found in science fiction. He attributes her relative lack of popularity as a contemporary writer to her motives for writing: "she didn't write for the modern, Marxist-oriented critic" but instead for ordinary readers who enjoy good stories well told. That Marion Zimmer Bradley never dedicated one of her novels to Brackett is, she says, one of her deepest regrets: "I waited too long; I was waiting for something good enough, a novel *worthy* of being dedicated to Leigh."

It is not fair to say that Brackett suffered from absolute critical neglect, for I know of about 125 reviews and pieces of criticism that mention her or her work. *The Science Fiction Encyclopedia* contains a sizable entry about her, gives her credit for influencing Bradbury, and notes that Edmond Hamilton's work "improved sharply in quality" after their marriage. Magill's *Survey of Science Fiction Literature* contains essays on two of her novels; Gregg Press has reprinted *The Sword of Rhiannon* in hardcover with a respectable introduction by Elizabeth Lynn; and a comprehensive bibliography of works by and about her makes up part of one volume in G. K. Hall's "Masters of Science

Fiction and Fantasy" series. But the feeling remains that these are not enough.

And that feeling can be substantiated. When Algis Budrys reviewed *The Best of Leigh Brackett* in December 1977, he strongly implied that the extent and value of her influence on and insights into science fiction—its recent history, its theory, its practice—have been great indeed. How great, and how respected and beloved she was, found storybook expression almost simultaneously with her death. Having visited with her frequently during the preceding months and weeks, Harlan Ellison knew that the script for Lucas still required some polishing. When he learned that she was dead, he resolved that she have the posthumous honor of being the sole credited author of the screenplay. He called George Lucas immediately, offered to polish the script anonymously and without a fee, and discovered that Ray Bradbury and Michael Moorcock had each called hours before, each having made the identical offer. The Queen of Space Opera was a woman who evoked a sense of wonder in her personal relations as well as with her works.

"Sense of wonder" is science fiction's analogue of mainstream literature's "shock of recognition." The latter phrase was coined by Herman Melville in writing about Nathaniel Hawthorne's fiction; it describes the experience of reading and being almost overcome by the sudden discovery of the genius bursting forth. There can be no great literature without this attribute, for it is that which gets to readers, that which enables them to know the potential in humankind, to glimpse for an instant the true reflection of their actual and possible selves, and to perceive momentarily the miraculous reality of the cosmos.

Leigh Brackett practiced that magic. Consciously or by some way letting the unconscious slip into her awareness, she put words together so that they created something new and real even as they described what never would or even could exist. In her introduction to *The Best of Planet Stories No. 1*, not only does she justify "space opera" (usually a derogatory term for science fiction/fantasy tales that intellectuals find too heroic or adventure filled); she actually evokes the sense of wonder that she is describing.

> The tale of adventure—of great courage and daring, of battle against the forces of darkness and the unknown—has been with the human race

since it first learned to talk. It began as part of the primitive survival technique, interwoven with magic and ritual, to explain and propitiate the vast forces of nature with which man could not cope in any other fashion. . . .

The so-called space opera is the folk-tale, the hero-tale, of our own particular niche in history. No more than a few years back, Goddard had to pretend that his rockets were for high-altitude research only because he was afraid to use the word "space." The important men, who were carrying their brains in their hip pockets, continued to sit upon them, sneering, until Sputnik went up and frightened the daylights out of them. But the space opera has been telling us tales of spaceflight, of journeys to other worlds in this solar system, even to other galaxies. . . . These stories served to stretch our little minds, to draw us out beyond our narrow skies into the vast glooms of interstellar space, where the great suns ride in splendor and the bright nebulae fling their veils of fire parsecs long across the universe; where the Coal-sack and the Horsehead make patterns of black mystery; where the Cepheid variables blink their evil eyes and a billion nameless plants may harbor life-forms infinitely numerous and strange.*

We could discuss this passage in terms of parallelism, periodic sentences, order of climax, and the like; or we can simply read it and be moved. Choosing the latter does not preclude rereading the passage and realizing that Brackett's words do not create a fiction but render marvelous what we admit as fact. Now, if we turn to her fiction, at least we are prepared.

The Long Tomorrow (1955) is generally considered the best of Brackett's longer works. It is speculative fiction, not science fantasy or space opera, set in the agricultural midwest after our technomaniacal propensities have run their course and reduced the United States to a number of isolated pockets of small towns and surrounding farmlands. The survivors, modeled on people like the Mennonites, are fearful of anything even reminiscent of preholocaust technology. Religious before, they react to the "destruction" remembered by grandparents as the final warning: God allowed the cities and all they represent to be destroyed because, obviously, God was more than a little displeased with the lives of city dwellers, scientists, and others who had evidently chosen the way of Satan. Persons in any way oriented toward progress

---

* From the introduction to *The Best of Planet Stories #1*, edited by Leigh Brackett. Copyright © 1975 by Random House, Inc. Reprinted by permission of Ballantine Books, a Division of Random House, Inc.

(a reconstruction of the evil past) were treated as heretics, even to the point of public executions.

The maturation of the third generation of survivors coincided with a natural increase in population, greater contact with other groups who had survived, and, consequentially, with the practicality of more complex social and economic structures. Common sense suggested commercial growth and a mitigation of the harsh laws that prohibited it. But those of the cities had been deluded by what seemed common sense to them, and the religious mind could easily imagine what that "common sense" would spawn. Thus an artifact like an operable radio was a tool of Satan to be destroyed; books from the old time (most of them religious) were burned or hidden away; and anyone who wanted to regain the knowledge of the past, especially if connected in some way with Bartorstown (where scientists allegedly had isolated themselves), was obviously the anti-Christ himself.

The protagonist of the novel, an adolescent chafing at the repressions and arch conservatism of his upbringing, actually escapes from home and, in time, arrives at the fabled Bartorstown. It does exist. It is populated by real scientists and their supporters, a community of people obsessed by their quest for control over nuclear power, in awe of the nuclear reactor they have (which may or may not yield up the secret of negating the terrifying potentialities of the atom), and who jealously venerate what may be the only operating computer on the planet. Not surprisingly, Bartorstown security is, if anything, stricter than the midwestern theocratic dicta.

Brackett manages the novel beautifully. She concentrates on the initiation into maturity of her protagonist and fleshes out the more important characters he encounters. Her prose is subdued, her plot as simple as her subject allows, and her implied thematic statements deliberately ambivalent. This last is especially noteworthy, for she presents both the agrarian reactionaries and the science-centered technocrats *fairly*. While the God-fearing majority is patently wrong in its reactions to changing social conditions, its basic values—caution about technological excess, respect for the spiritual aspects of humankind— are self-evidently right. At the same time, we sense the importance of the scientists' dream but realize also that their zeal and single mindedness have imposed an inhumane regimentation upon the citizens of Bartorstown, who may not leave the place until they have been judged absolutely loyal to its ideals.

Despite its low-key narration, *The Long Tomorrow* does impart a sense of wonder. After reading the novel, having experienced the lure and the repulsion of both social alternatives, we come slowly to an understanding of great magnitude: even in *speculation* about the challenges faced by survivors of a nuclear war, there is no answer simpler than "human nature," and that is not a simple answer at all. In addition, Brackett's novel is realistically predictive in a startling, eye-opening way. Since it was published in 1955, it had to have been written earlier; even if we discount the obvious care that must have structured the novel, it still takes months to make a manuscript into a book. As recently as August 1981, when CBS televised a five-part report on our national defense, the Canadian role in NORAD was barely mentioned. If television viewers are left ignorant of matters twenty-five years old, it is extremely unlikely that Leigh Brackett was privy to the "several years of collaboration" with Canada that led to the institution of the North American Air Defense Command. The wonder? The uncanny "prediction"? Bartorstown was hidden in the Rockies, in an area accessible if one follows the Platte River upstream. Not until 1957 did NORAD come to be, and its headquarters (mainly underground) are located in Colorado Springs. Check a map.

For a writer who emphatically expressed her dislike for heavy thematic elements in fiction as early as 1942 and who by 1975 had articulated her distaste for them by the epithet "Big Thinks," Brackett seems out of character as author of *The Long Tomorrow*. She is, but only because of her subdued tone. What Brackett deprecates, I think, is the dependence on thematic statements that renders what could have been a literary work into a tract and causes characters never to do more than utter an author's favorite platitudes. *The Long Tomorrow* made its point so emphatically "back when it counted" because its author would not be satisfied unless its theme grew naturally from the actions of well-developed characters in a solid, believable setting.

Brackett also revealed her dislike of heavy-handed moralizing in two of her shorter works, in which we never feel the gravity of theme until we read the conclusion of the adventures. One story, "The Tweener" (1955), involves the interactions among the members of a typical American family and the rabbit-sized Martian mammal that (Uncle) Fred brought back for the children. Matt, the children's father, feels a wave of apprehension even before the tweener is taken from its traveling box. But the children love the furry little critter, name it "John Carter" (they've read Burroughs, too), and soon can hardly be pried away from it. Lucille, Matt's wife and Fred's sister, is maternally tolerant: the pet seems to make the children so happy. Still apprehensive, Matt gets headaches, alternates between insomnia and nightmares, and becomes thoroughly distraught. Because John Carter is native to a cold planet (though he had been kept inside the Mars base by Fred to acclimate him to Earth temperatures and atmosphere), the root cellar becomes his home. (Yet, "it" becomes "he": "John Carter" develops rapidly from the pet to a person.) On one occasion he burrows out into the back yard, but he is returned safely to his "room" and the hole he dug covered by a large, heavy stone. Things are all right, except for Matt's continuing problems.

Finally, unable any longer to endure the headaches, feelings of unease, and "dim sad dreams of loss and yearning," Matt kills the tweener and makes it appear that John Carter had dug out again and had been met by an unfriendly canine. The story makes it plain that xenophobia had been prevalent among the humans on Mars and almost implies that it is the sole cause of Matt's uneasiness with the Martian native. But, after reading the story a few times, we realize that the children's fascination and Matt's nightmares share the same source: John Carter is evidently a telepath, returning and evoking the children's innocent friendliness and affection but "telling the truth" to Matt, whose antipathy Carter has felt from the beginning and whose world is for the Martian a hot and humid and even physically oppressive environment.

The other story, "All the Colors of the Rainbow" (1957), is similar. Aliens from Galactic Center arrive on the fringe world we call Earth and, after the proper political civilities are exchanged and the Americans in the story know that they will get weather control, at least, from the interstellar alliance, Flin and his permanent mate Ruvi drive an automobile away from the cities, "to get out and see the country [and] to learn what [Earth] people are really like." They certainly learn. Their main problem is that, to the rural folk they encounter, they are "green niggers" and, because they are colored, they are treated, ultimately, the way the Klan has treated black ones. At least Flin and Ruvi survive.

Flin is an expert weather controller; he had worked at stabilizing the atmospheres of several other worlds and had taken the job on far-off Earth so that with the extra pay he and Ruvi could afford to marry.

The first sentence of the story is retrospective: "It had rained in the valley, steadily and hard, for thirty-six hours."

Neither of these stories has a "Big Think," but each of them contains a good many little feelings. "All the Colors of the Rainbow" is blatantly antiracist, but it refuses to yield to the kind of logical analysis that could, with satisfaction, be called a clear theme. What is done to Ruvi and Flin is evil, but the country folk were acting from fear, not ideology; the same is true of the demise of John Carter, for Matt is terrified nearly to psychosis by the little alien. What is striking about both these stories is that Flin's and the Martian's inflictions of pain upon humans has no moral justification. Brackett handles what is usually thinly disguised rationalization (the conscious mind at work) as the complex head-*and-heart* responses of sentient beings made irrationally to suffer: the victims of human hostility are no more "right" in their vengeance than the hostile humans who stimulated it. Because of fear and ignorance, panic and adrenaline (or its alien equivalent), bad things happen and only in later, calmer moments are we able to judge—instead of feel—that they are evil. When we first read "The Tweener," we feel that Matt is wrong; when we first read "All the Colors of the Rainbow," we feel that Flin is right. Upon further reflection, though, we are very likely to think and feel differently. With these two stories as only partial evidence, we must credit Brackett with the remarkable ability to create little worlds with large complexities, to use ordinary English—clear, crisp, at times brutal—which, after we have read it, leaves us with a sense of wonder that we cannot resolve the problems set up by her prose even as it reaches aesthetically satisfying conclusions.

One of Brackett's traits was her incurable romanticism. I suspect that phrase means that she just could not help writing about heroic deeds performed by characters who thrived on challenges in settings of dangerous, exotic beauty. But to be fair, we can also let "romanticism" mean the conscious refusal to be cynical. In 1969 Brackett identified the worst attribute of contemporary science fiction—and "mainstream" fiction, too—as its "loss of splendor. And this at a time when man stands . . . with all the universe before him!" In *The Secret of Sinharat* (1964), Stark's response to the offer of never-ending life is a silent pause, a shake of the head, and "I don't think so. Life has not been so soft and sweet for me that I would want to live it over." Perhaps it is romantic, perhaps not, to write of splendid deeds and places; it seems that, by keeping human mortality always visible in the backgrounds of her fictions, Brackett adheres to the real and at the same time captures the essence of heroism; the mortal human being, accepting a possibly fatal challenge, risks failure and death. Without those risks, life would become a meaningless game, for if we do not win the first time, we can play again: repeatedly, unendingly, inhumanly.

Another characteristic is her infrequent use of feminine characters, sometimes criticized as antifeminist, sometimes explained away by the dominantly masculine audience for whom she wrote. Brackett is supposed to have said that she would let no woman into a story unless the woman was there to "*do* something." As early as 1944 she created one of the considerable number of "Brackett women":

> She was tall. She was built and muscled like a lioness, and she walked with a flat-hipped arrogance. . . . Her eyes were blue, hot and bright, [and she was dressed] in a leather kilt and sandals, her magnificent body bare above the waist. She carried a longsword slung across her back, the hilt standing above the left shoulder. She had been using it. Her skin was smeared with blood and grime. There was a long cut on her thigh and another across her flat belly, and a bitter weariness lay on her like a burden in spite of her denial of it.

Beudag the Venusian, the woman who was just described, is certainly intended to evoke a feeling of sexual attraction from the men who read about her, but most of those 1940s men—if they met women like Beudag in real life—would fear rather than respect such strength and courage, would find the musculature and marks of battle off-putting rather than sexually alluring. Present-day feminists—men as well as women—can find in "Brackett women" the feminine counterparts to Stark.

A third trait is Brackett's continuing development of Eric John Stark, a man whose boyhood was spent with the native Mercurian subhumans, whose genetic heritage was Earthly, and whose psyche never really adapted to the niceties of civilization. Stark, the orphaned boy, was N'Chaka, the man without a tribe; Stark, the adult, is a mercenary, but he earns his wages fighting for the barbarian natives of worlds being exploited by intruders. He is a renegade, successful in his flights from legal justice, and he honors only the laws of his own nature: respect for life and love and friendship, for courage, honesty, and even cunning when it is not deceit. He is an ideal, it is true, but one that makes plain Brackett's full appreciation of humanity; persons like Stark are rare but, to those who do not fear to know themselves and others, inestimably attractive because of their acceptance of their "animal" as well as their "higher" natures.

Brackett never tired of Stark; he appeared first in "Queen of the Martian Catacombs" then in "Enchantress of Venus" (both 1949) and in "Black Amazon of Mars" (1951). We may notice that these titles— which may have been Brackett's or those of the editor of *Planet Stories*— emphasize the feminine, and then try to make of that whatever can be made. The two tales set on Mars were expanded to novel length and published in 1964 as *The Secret of Sinharat* and *People of the Talisman*. Ellison's forthcoming *The Last Dangerous Visions* prompted the reappearance of Brackett's hero in "Stark and the Star Kings" and that, in turn, led her to write *The Ginger Star*, *The Hounds of Skaith* (both 1974), and *The Reavers of Skaith* (1976), the trilogy (almost tetralogy) I mentioned much earlier.

Finally, we must note the eminent lucidity and grace of Brackett's prose. They make her settings credible and solid, they make her characters unforgettable, they make one know what Algis Budrys meant when he said that "Leigh was the best then, and she is the best now." We should, as a matter of principle, contest that overstatement; in order to do so, though, we need to read and/or reread a generous sampling of her work. Whatever the verdict pronounced afterward, it will in one way or other echo the words of Lester del Rey: "Thank you, Leigh Brackett."

2

Patricia Mathews

C. L. MOORE'S CLASSIC SCIENCE FICTION

Catherine L. Moore is best known for the short stories "Shambleau," "Vintage Season," and "No Woman Born"; the novel *Judgment Night*, and the Jirel of Joiry series. "Vintage Season" and "No Woman Born" are hard science fiction as is *Judgment Night*; "Shambleau" is science fiction with overtones of myth; Jirel of Joiry is frank fantasy.

Whether science fiction or fantasy, short story or novel, these works all share a set of definable and complex values reflected in complex, tightly crafted, often surprising plots. The plots are built around themes of some depth that Moore either invented or was the first to explore to such an extent. The writing itself is designed to appeal to all of the senses, especially the visual. Moore has said "I love description and colorful adjectives. My stories have always needed pruning and cutting in the rewrite," and adds, "I do think in three dimensions."

Beyond that, several of her works, particularly Jirel of Joiry, are given added depth by the fact that the adventures take place not only in a real or fantasy world, but also within the leading character's soul. The stakes are high, and the battles are both real and extremely important, wherever they take place.

"Shambleau," Moore's first story, is the now-classic tale of frontiersman Northwest Smith's encounter with a frightened, helpless alien who is running from a boomtown lynch mob. What the alien, Shambleau, is and why the mob wants to lynch her, are the secrets of the story, and Moore's answer is neither simple nor obvious.

"Vintage Season," a much later short story, also has a mystery at its heart. A group of decadent, eccentric tourists arrive in an unnamed town at an unnamed, but clearly present, time and wait. Wait for what? Where are they from? More important, what is their purpose?

"No Woman Born" is the story of the once-great dancer Dierdre, fatally injured in a theater fire, whose only chance for life is to be given a cyborg body—robot in form but controlled by her own mind.

Judgment Night is a novel of political intrigue. An empire is about to fall to invaders from without, and a conspiracy of its own subjects is about to take place from within. The elder gods, who explicitly say the subjects cannot be trusted, are standing by with oracles, one of which may prove fatal. And perhaps nonhumans are waiting in the background to pick up the pieces.

The Jirel of Joiry series take place in what may be ninth-century southern France. The Lady Jirel rides to war at the head of her troops and leads her soldiers into battle, but when her wars involve the supernatural, she battles alone.

Moore's love of description can be seen in her word pictures of the writhing scarlet tendrils of the alien Shambleau, the golden beauty of the reborn Dierdre, the bleak and beautiful imagery throughout *Judgment Night*, and the grim, sometimes lush underworld settings in which Jirel fights her lonely battles. It reaches a peak in "Vintage Season," where the reader can smell and taste the wine, feel the strange set of the clothing on the tourists' bodies, and where the wordless confrontation between the tourist and her contemporary landlady is experienced on the emotional, not visual, level.

> Science fiction is a romance of the machine. Fantasy is a romance of the soul.
>
> C. J. Cherryh

Judgment Night is a battles-and-spaceships novel of hard science fiction. "No Woman Born" is a robot story; "Shambleau" can be considered a simple adventure. What gives them depth is the component Cherryh mentions, the battles that take place in the soul.

In "Shambleau," Northwest Smith has found that a simple act of decency—rescuing the victim of a lynch mob—has led him into a horrifying addiction of a psychic, quasisexual nature, for Shambleau is not what she seems. Once she has embraced him, "through all that was Smith the dreadful pleasure ran. And it was truly dreadful. Dimly he knew it, even as his body answered to the root deep ecstasy." But although the problem set by the story can be defined as "What is a Shambleau?" and "Can Smith get out of this trap, and how?", it does not end there. It ends with Smith's response to his partner's demand that he shoot to kill the next time he sees one of the things—the Shambleau—that so nearly destroyed him.

> Smith's eyes, pale and resolute as steel, met Yarol's levelly.
> "I'll—try," he said. And his voice wavered.

"No Woman Born" is also a story of a battle within the soul, both for the dancer, Dierdre, and for her friends. It is told from the viewpoint of Dierdre's best friend and manager John Harris. It begins as simple concern for the injured, rebuilt Dierdre and covers every possible re-action to robots, androids, or cyborgs, later explored in greater detail by Isaac Asimov. First, the frightened Harris envisions a clunking body or brain in a case, and his reaction is pity. Then, when he sees Dierdre, he is terrified that the world will not accept her in her new guise. Her doctor, Malzer, fears she will be cut off from humanity, lacking all but two of the human senses.

". . . She isn't a human being any more, and I think what humanity is left in her will drain out little by little and never be replaced."

But with Dierdre's remarkably successful comeback, the Franken-stein complex sets in and Malzer determines to stop—to kill—her; but, being human, he must confront her first. And Dierdre, being human, answers with reason. Pamela Sargent comments:

> Moore's story is an important one for several reasons. . . it is one of the earliest thoughtful treatments of the cyborg, a person who is partly or mostly machine. Dierdre, in her metal body, has gained new senses to replace the ones she lost (smell, taste, and touch), and she recognizes that she could easily become alienated from the human beings around her. She thinks she can prevent this from happening by using the contact with her audience provided by dancing. The men in the story feel sorry for her, seeing her somehow as trapped and cut off in her mechanical body. Dierdre, however, finds a new perceptual world opening up to her, and succeeds in creating a new style of dance as well.

The struggle within the souls of her friends is explicit. The tale of her own struggles is implicit in every confrontation shown between Dierdre, on the one hand, and her friends, on the other. She now has totally unexpected powers and capacities, and as she reminds her friends, "My brain's human, and no human brain could leave such possibilities untested." Yet, she herself must accept her powers, relate them to her humanity, and somehow deal as an equal with those who cannot follow where she goes. She knows it to be a hard, perhaps impossible task, although she can do nothing else but try. Everyone who has ever found herself venturing where her family or old friends cannot follow can immediately identify.

Judgment Night ties the struggle within the soul of Juille of Ericon to the fate of the empire whose heart is Ericon, for in this story, the land and the ruler are one. On one level, *Judgment Night* is a decline-and-fall-of-empire story. On the same level, parallel to the political story, it is the story of Juille's maturing, too little and too late. In this, the most fatalistic of Moore's works, every error of values has fatal consequences for the entire human race, for Ericon is at war in a highly technological society.

"How much of civilization do you think would survive any such holocaust as that?" Juille's father, the elderly and semiretired emperor, asks as they discuss the imminent war. "It would mean our ruin even if we won."

But Juille, hotheaded, stubborn, warrior-trained, and explicitly cited as a fair sample of her culture, answers, "As long as I can, the Empire is ours. I won't share it with those hairy savages." Her basic position is, "I'd have wiped them out. . . if it meant the end of the empire. . . I'll do it yet—by the Hundred Emperors I will!"

As the war grows more and more imminent, breaks out, and then progresses, Juille is given a series of decisions to make, not just practical ones, but key policy decisions that must be informed by her basic values. She must choose whether or not to use a weapon that hunts down and kills an individual, and that once set cannot be recalled; whether to negotiate to stop the war; and if to use her weapon, on whom. Juille's basic policy is not working. Her people are losing the war. If it can't be won, can it be stopped?

Judgment Night was copyrighted in 1943, at the height of World War II. Its antiwar theme, its sense that both sides are equally right or equally wrong, seems to belong either to an earlier or to a later date. Yet the fatalism, the sense that civilization is sliding down into darkness and that the human race may well be finished, reflects the reality of the period as in a mirror.

Judgment Night is science fiction. The Jirel of Joiry series is fantasy. The battles within the soul of Juille, in *Judgment Night*, were explicit: Juille must make a decision. They paralleled the battles in the real world and were the cause of some real-world battles, and the effect of others. The battles Jirel fights are against magic, using her sword or her wits as weapons. Yet, in a deeper and more allegorical sense, the battles all take place within her soul, symbolically. This is most clearly seen in Moore's first, and many say finest, Jirel story, "Black God's Kiss."

Marion Zimmer Bradley interprets the theme of "Black God's Kiss" as one of rape, vengeance, and guilt. "Jirel, in men's clothing [is] dragged before the conqueror, Guillaume. He has her unarmored, and contemptuously kisses her." Bradley is of the opinion: "In 1978, a writer as honest as Moore would have given this contemptuous act its full weight: rape. In 1937, that was completely impossible. I don't think anyone who read the story then even thought in those terms; but the fantasy element was there covert but unmistakeable."

She continues the plot summary:

> Jirel, burning with rage and shame, goes into a hidden room beneath her chapel, which contains an entryway to an alien land; looking not for escape, to which the priest counsels her, but for revenge. After many terrifying adventures, she comes into the temple of the "black God" focused entirely on the God's figure, his mouth, strangely, puckered to receive a kiss; Jirel, receiving the kiss, struggles back to the real world, drooping and dying under the weight of the kiss; and when she emerges from the underworld, bestows the kiss in turn upon the troubled Guillaume; who, under its dreadful bane, collapses and dies on the spot. And Jirel, stricken with anguish, knows that "there is no light for her anywhere in the world" now that Guillaume, the beloved and the ravisher, is dead.

On the one hand, as a tale of violation and revenge, it ends with the usual Moore note of reversal—Northwest Smith, unable to promise to destroy Shambleau; Dierdre, saying "I wonder," with a distant metallic note in her voice—Moore's heroes go through with what they started but with full awareness of the cost. Jirel's regrets seem to be easily explained in terms of simple human guilt rather than identification with the oppressor or love of the ravisher; Jirel, the warrior, has killed before but not like this; and Guillaume is a man she could have, in other circumstances, liked.

Still, the story is not about magic, the supernatural, or swordplay. It is about violation, revenge, and guilt and is a battle in and of the soul; that is what makes it more than "sword and sorcery," makes it great fantasy.

"Black God's Shadow," the sequel to "Black God's Kiss," is about expiation, laying guilt to rest, and the high cost of hatred. Jirel, haunted by the ghost of Guillaume, ventures again into the underworld where the black god lives and where Guillaume's ghost cries pitifully. At long last, again after many terrifying adventures, she comes upon an object that is "all the ugliness of Guillaume—she saw it as she stared. All his cruelty and arrogance and brutish force. The image might have been a picture of Guillaume's sins, with just enough of his virtues left in to point its dreadfulness."

More horrible than that is the realization that the best in Guillaume is chained to this beast, " . . . so just, yet so infinitely unjust . . . the very fineness of him was a weapon to torture his soul, turned against him even as his sins were turned."

Jirel weeps, and in weeping, melts the black god's spell, returning to a realization of her own warmth and life; with this weeping, she is now able to fight the god and to follow Guillaume's ghost, until in a blaze of life, she lays it to rest and finds the peace within herself that she had given him at last.

The later Jirel of Joiry stories read as if they were written earlier, for they return to a simpler beginning of Jirel's quest. The next story in the series, "Jirel Meets Magic," is about growing up. Jirel, behaving like any young warrior, storms into the castle of the wizard Giraud, determined to kill him for ambushing ten of her followers. She follows him through a window in the castle that leads to a strange land and comes upon a strange, queenly woman, Jarisme, who is torturing a dying dryad, Irsla, for defying her. The wizard Giraud is one of Jarisme's servants; Jarisme is the enemy Jirel must defeat.

Three things are notable about Jarisme as a foe. The first encounter between soldier and sorceress takes place on an almost childish level, a matter of snotty insults and dirty looks like a pair of schoolchildren about to fight. Jarisme, who punished the disobedience of Irsla, the dryad, so cruelly, stays her hand for Jirel with no visible reason. Why?

Jirel wonders. Why had she not been slain as Irsla was slain, for defiance of this queer land's ruler? And Jarisme's magic, in the long run, is the sort that would be good for Jirel and her maturing.

Jarisme has the power to send Jirel from world to world, and Jirel is whisked through many strange worlds where she meets many strange beasts, some of them incarnations of Jarisme herself. At last, in Jarisme's hall, Jirel is present at a worship service where the alien inhabitants of these worlds are the congregation and Jarisme is the priestess. Here, by Jarisme's magic, Jirel's whole life is spread out before her timelessly—past and present coexisting in one eternal moment, in all their original emotional intensity. It is almost too much for Jirel to bear. What saves Jirel is her own natural rage, "Rage at life for permitting such pain to be. Rage at Jarisme for forcing her into such memory." In this rebellion, "her own violence had melted the spell by which Jarisme held her."

Jarisme's tower world breaks, and Jirel is returned to the world outside the wizard's window. The wizard lives, a mean, petty, mocking man. Jirel kills him and goes back to her own dimension. It is unlikely she has gone back unchanged.

So Jirel, an unthinking young warrior on a simple quest, meets a magician who shows her the infinite variety of worlds, then forces her to confront herself and her life in all its nakedness, and finally goads her into a rebellion—a self-assertion—which is the only thing that can free her from the spell laid on her by her own past. In this, Jarisme is mentor, not enemy, for all her mockery and seeming cruelty. She may also be seen as a personification of Jirel's own past, a part of herself, which must be overcome before she can take the next step. But once again, in this, she has acted as mentor, not as foe.

Jirel's next encounter is with an adversary totally traditional in women's experience, the domineering male who will have her at all costs. Pav, King of Romne, at the very beginning of "The Dark Land" speaks. "There is in you a hot and savage strength which no other woman in any land I know possesses. A force to match my own, Lady Jirel. None but you is fit to be my queen. *So I have taken you for my own.*"

The problem for Jirel is how to resist and escape, for as she tells the Lady Death, "I am not a woman to be taken against her will, and Pav is no choice of mine."

In this, as in the Black God stories, Jirel's struggle is to maintain her own integrity in a world in which she is regarded, qua woman, as prey. Her method is direct. Force having failed her, she makes common cause with Lady Death of the Dark Lands, Pav's consort queen. Upon learning that the nameless corpse-witch does not love Pav, she offers, "Let me slay Pav as I set out to do, and leave this land kingless, for your rule alone." But there is neither land nor king in Pav's realm, for "the Darkness was Romne, and Romne was Pav," and in destroying Pav, Jirel destroyed the Dark Land as well.

C. L. Moore wrote two other Jirel stories, both after her collaboration with Henry Kuttner had begun. One, "Quest of the Starstone," is a collaboration with Kuttner. The other, "Hellsgarde," was written independently. "Hellsgarde" is the tale of a haunted castle and the eccentric, ghoulish people who hang around, waiting for the ghost of the villainous Andred. It is also the tale of a box that Jirel's enemy, Guy of Garlot, covets. The box contains Andred's treasure, but the ghouls have warned her not to open it. "Hellsgarde" is a very effective horror story, and it is a pleasure to see how much more subtle Jirel has become in letting her enemies bring their own punishment down on their heads, rather than slashing out with her sword.

This was C. L. Moore's last Jirel of Joiry tale.

Whether science fiction or fantasy, short story or novel, these works by C. L. Moore all share a set of definable and complex values reflected in their plots. First among these values is her basic belief that people's actions matter. All the battles Jirel of Joiry fights are won by her own actions, directly, as when she fights her way out of a trap ("Hellsgarde") or, indirectly, when she enlists an ally, whose actions help her in victory ("The Dark Land"). In "Vintage Season," what the tourists do, or deliberately refrain from doing, have the harshest of consequences. In "No Woman Born," the entire issue is what Harris will do, what Malzer will do, and most of all, what Dierdre will do. Even in *Judgment Night*, the most fatalistic of all Moore's works, in which every plan comes to disaster, the defeats are based on the failure of human beings to make the right decisions and to do the right thing, not on whim or chance or a malignant or playful universe.

Not only do people's actions matter, but in Moore's universe, victory is possible, given will, intelligence, and strength. Jirel of Joiry triumphs, always, by her own efforts. Dierdre, in "No Woman Born," succeeds in making a metal body her own, and she succeeds against all odds, in her chosen profession after her return as a cyborg. Victory is not inevitable—this is not Hollywood—but even in defeat, we feel that it is still possible. Oliver, in "Vintage Season," has desperately tried to warn his contemporaries of the disasters the tourists know of but are bound by oath not to speak of. He is too sick to succeed. Here, realistically, is a portrait of someone who has done his best according to his or anybody's standards but was defeated by forces too strong for him. Yet, in another, less overpowering disaster, Oliver might well have succeeded; the story is tragic, but not defeatist. Likewise, Juille in *Judgment Night* fails because, while she tried her best, her best was informed by tragically wrongheaded values. Had she made other choices, she could have saved civilization, if not her empire. Victory is possible, if not inevitable.

To C. L. Moore, abilities, intelligence, and strength are un-qualified good; evil only comes with the misuse of these abilities. Jirel's strength and fighting spirit are repeatedly spoken of with respect and admiration, by her enemies and by her people. Pav of Romne wants her for his bride because of these qualities. Nobody, in the harshest of exchange of insults, finds them anything but good.

Similarly, nothing is said against either the intelligence or the fighting spirit of Juille of Ericon in *Judgment Night*. Ericon is a formerly patriarchal society abruptly turned egalitarian, to the extent that women have been fully included in its warrior ethos. Juille rages to her father, "If I were a man, maybe you'd listen to me." But nobody suggests that Juille would be better off if she were less intelligent or less of a warrior. The constant thread running throughout *Judgment Night* of Juille's need to learn to be a woman as well as a warrior is a recurring plea for her to expand her behavioral and emotional repertoire before her one-sidedness brings disaster on the entire empire. She has a preteener's one-sided outlook on these matters:

"To her mind, indeed, a woman was much more suited to uniform than a man, so easily can she throw off all hampering civilian ideas once she gives her full loyalty to a cause. . . . for those women who still clung to the old standards, Juille felt a sort of tolerant contempt. But they made her uneasy, too." She has yet to reach the simple acceptance of her sexuality that Jirel of Joiry and Dierdre display. But what she does have is considered good. It is just not enough.

Evil in *Judgment Night* comes from an adult's intelligence and training used by someone with the all-or-nothing values of an adolescent who misuses her talents to the wrong ends. Evil in Jirel of Joiry comes from abilities in magic or on the battlefield turned toward evil ends or, less frequently, from the mindlessness of beasts. Evil in "Vintage Season" comes from what intelligence the tourists do have and the great abilities of the artist Cenbe, turned toward a conscientious failure to act. "Kleph's race were spectators." Evil in "No Woman Born" is a product of panic, of failure to think, when Malzer in one mad moment decides that Dierdre must be stopped—a euphemism for killed—but Dierdre's abilities are entirely praiseworthy. There is a strong hint that her friends and her audience loved her for her former abilities and for the new ones she displays in her metal body on the dance stage. Not even Malzer in the throes of his Frankenstein complex finds her new strength and new senses evil nor does he fear she will misuse them. His only fear, and hers, is that with so few sensory experiences in common with flesh and blood humanity, she may lose touch. It is a risk she accepts.

The value of alliance, and friendship, is clearly shown in Moore's writing. Northwest Smith of "Shambleau" is rescued by his sidekick, Yarol. Dierdre is kept alive and sane by the love of her friends and audiences. Oliver and Sue stand together against the tourists in "Vintage Season," and Oliver's defeat may in part be due to the breaking of that alliance by his attraction to the outtimer, Kleph.

Alliance and friendship is shown to be a value, even in tales of those lone operators, Juille of Ericon and Jirel of Joiry. Juille is a loner, by choice, and becomes more and more isolated as she goes further and further down the wrong road in an ever-increasing vicious spiral. Her two genuinely close relationships were with her tutor, Helia, where the bond was broken by political developments in which Juille herself had an indirect hand, and with her father, where there was a weakly formed bond. If the latter had been stronger, much of Juille's wrongheadedness could have been prevented; her father made good sense.

Jirel of Joiry, again, works alone. She has no best friend or partner. But Jirel is surrounded by people who love her and will back her in any enterprise—from her priest to her maidservants to her men-at-arms—just as she will back them. In one adventure, "The Dark Land," she saves herself by suggesting an alliance to a woman who is there already; the woman accepts, and they both prevail.

Finally, implicit in all Moore's work is a feeling that the universe basically makes sense and can be dealt with. It can be terrifying, as in some of the other dimensions Jirel of Joiry visits. It can be set in motion against humanity and humanity's current plans, as in *Judgment Night*. It may be more eccentric than anyone supposes, again as in the Jirel stories. But it is not irrational, and it is not incomprehensible; it is just full of as-yet unknowns. There is a race that serves as gods to the empire in *Judgment Night*; they are openly not to be trusted. Humanity is to trust its own judgment in the last analysis. It does not, and judgment falls like the working out of a law of nature. There is magic in Jirel's world, but she treats it as moderns do machines that they have not studied but do recognize. "Jirel shrugged after a moment's bewilderment. She had met magic before."

There is a clarity to all Moore's writing that comes out most clearly in her visual imagery, a delight in the senses, and in awareness, in abilities and the use of the abilities, in a world where people matter and their choices are important, where victory is possible, and the bonds between people help make it possible—this is the romance of C. L. Moore's soul.

Roger C. Schlobin

ANDRE NORTON:
Humanity Amid the Hardware

Andre Norton (born 1912), along with C. L. Moore, Leigh Brackett, and Judith Merril, began an explosion of women science fiction writers in the 1950s that is still continuing. Norton and her fellow pioneers opened the way for the many major writers that have followed. Norton, however, has had a far more varied writing career than many of her colleagues and has appealed to a wider spectrum of readers. She was incorrectly known primarily as a juvenile writer by some (a career she did consider when she began to write), but her numerous adventure stories have pleased readers of all ages for over forty-five years and continue to do so. Evidence of this is the numerous librarians who testify to the high circulation of her works among children and adults and by the continual in-print status of large numbers of her works. The telltale observations are that readers of her gothics are often surprised that she writes science fiction, young people are stunned by her following among adults, and adults are astonished to discover her popularity among young people.

Andre Norton's literary career began in 1934 with her first publication, *The Prince Commands, Being the Sundry Adventures of Michael Karl, Sometime Crown Prince & Pretender to the Throne of Morvania*, a juvenile historical novel. In 1938 she published *Ralestone Luck*, another historical adventure for younger readers. These two novels marked Norton's legal name change from her birth name of Mary Alice to Andre, a change occasioned by her planned entry into the male-dominated field of juvenile adventure fiction (not into science fiction) and inspired by her genuine affection for the name Andre. Thus, the many citations to "Andre" as a pseudonym are incorrect.*

Having produced some ninety-eight novels, thirty short stories, six collections, seven edited anthologies, numerous book reviews, non-fiction writing, and three poems, Norton is now entering her fifth decade of writing an unusual variety of fiction. Just a brief look at her book publications from 1979 to late 1981 reveals her varied abilities: *Seven Spells to Sunday*, a juvenile fantasy written in collaboration with Phyllis Miller; *Snow Shadow*, an adult gothic; *Star Ka'at and the Plant People*, juvenile science fiction written in collaboration with Dorothy Madlee and the third in a series; *Iron Butterflies*, an adult gothic; *Lore of the Witch World*, a collection of short stories and part of her famed fantasy series set on the Witch World; *Voorloper* and *Forerunner*, adult science fiction novels; and *Gryphon in Glory* and *Horn Crown*, two novels that are also part of the Witch World series.

The professional skills involved in such literary range are awesome. Yet, to a certain extent, they are predictable. Norton's rich and unusual childhood, which is detailed in this author's introduction to his *Andre Norton: A Primary and Secondary Bibliography*, provided her with the tools and disposition to pursue her career and avocation as a professional writer. Her mother, Bertha Stemm Norton (whose autobiography, *Bertie and May*, Andre finished and published in 1969), read to Andre before she could read herself. As a late child, born seventeen years after her sister, Andre developed relationships with her parents rather than with her contemporaries, and she benefited markedly from the greater sophistication and verbal skills her parents offered to her. Most significantly, her parents' book-rich home provided her with the life-long appetite for reading. Norton herself comments on this "curse" in her introduction to C. J. Cherryh's *Gate of Ivrel*:

> There are those among us who are compulsive readers—who will even settle a wandering eye on a scrap of newspaper on the bus floor if nothing better offers. Books flow in and out of our lives in an unending stream. Some we remember briefly, others bring us sitting upright, tense with suspense, our attention enthralled until the last word on the last page is digested. Then we step regretfully from the world that the author has

---

* The only pseudonyms she has ever used are "Andrew North" for three of the Solar Queen novels and "Allen Weston" in her collaboration with Grace Allen Hogarth for *Murders for Sale* (London: Hammond, 1954).

created, and we know that volume will be chosen to stand on already
too tightly packed shelves to be read again and again.

Among those authors whom Norton "read again and again" were
Edgar Rice Burroughs, H. Beam Piper, Dornford Yates (a pseudonym
for Cecil W. Mercer), Ruth Plumly Thompson, Talbot Mundy, William Hope Hodgson, and the nineteenth-century British novelists.
Their works are of particular note because they shaped her commitment
to the swiftly moving and entertaining plots that are so obvious in her
writing. In addition, Norton added to her affections a deep love for
thorough and meticulous research. A quick survey of the sources of
some of her science fiction novels reveals the erudition and scope of
her pursuits for backgrounds and accuracy. William Hope Hodgson's
The Nightland: A Love Tale (1912), a work she was instrumental in having
included in Lin Carter's Adult Fantasy Series, is the direct source for
Night of Masks. Norton's novel resulted from her fascination with Hodgson's future, sunless world; her modification was the innovative creation
of a world lit by an infrared sun. *Dark Piper* is based on the folktale
of the Pied Piper of Hamelin, and *Star Guard* includes a retelling of
Xenophon's *Anabasis*. The strange, oversized ring in *The Zero Stone* was
inspired by the description of an odd piece of jewelry, meant to be
worn over armor, in the off-beat *The Hock Shop* (1954) by Ralph Simp-
son, and its use is characteristic of the pieces of jewelry that frequently
occur in Norton's works as plot devices, symbols, and images. Her
Time War Novels—*The Time Traders*, *Galactic Derelict*, *The Defiant
Agents*, and *Key Out of Time*—are based on the meager history of the
prehistoric Beaker Traders as described in Paul Herrmann's *Conquest
by Man*. To convert a western into science fiction and write *The Beast
Master* and its sequel, *Lord of Thunder*, Norton consulted Navaho phrase
books and linguistic studies. *Merlin's Mirror*, like the juvenile fantasy
Steel Magic, was inspired by the Arthurian legends.

An additional major body of influence comes from Norton's skeptical
fascination with the pseudoscience psychometry. Psychometry is the
belief that physical objects retain memories of their pasts that can be
read by human sensitives. A good portion of her information about
this comes from the works of T. C. Lethbridge, notably *ESP: Beyond
Time and Distance*, *The Monkey's Tale: A Study in Evolution and Parapsy-
chology*, *A Step in the Dark*, and *The Legend of the Sons of God: A Fantasy?*
Psychometry is most obvious in Norton's *Forerunner Foray*, *Wraiths of*

Time, and the aforementioned *Merlin's Mirror*. Ziantha, the female protagonist of *Forerunner Foray*, demonstrates the nature of the pseudoscience as it functions in Norton's fiction:

> For a long time it had been a proven fact that any object wrought by
> intelligence (or even a natural stone or similar object that had been used
> for a definite purpose by intelligence) could record. From the fumbling
> beginnings of untrained sensitives, who had largely developed their own
> powers, much had been learned. It had been "magic" then; yet the talent
> was too "wild," because all men did not share it, and because it could
> not be controlled or used at will but came and went for reasons unknown
> to the possessors.

Interestingly, the belief that the power of the human mind can
plumb the depths of the memories contained in objects is a critical
element in understanding Norton's science fiction. Effective plotting
is her predominant stylistic skill, and her complete devotion to the
individual and the powers of the individual is the primary characteristic of her content. While hard science fiction writers like Larry
Niven and Hal Clement pursue the technologies of new ages and galactic interchange, Norton embraces and stresses an older, timeless view
in creating her characters. They are almost without exception portrayed
with compassion, producing a poignancy that Norton's readers have
long felt and loved. However, her affection does not extend to humankind and its products in general, and her novels are filled with the
evils of vast power structures and mindless, threatening forces—all
sadly human constructs. A sampling of a few titles affirms this.

In *Eye of the Monster*, the large evil forces are rampaging, reptilian
aliens and an apathetic Earth government. Automatic controls take the
three main characters on a blind flight to potential exile on a long-dead
planet in *Galactic Derelict*. *The Beast Master*'s young American Indian
protagonist must suffer in a society that neither understands nor cares
about him, and like many Norton protagonists, he finds empathy and
sympathy with aliens and animals. In the Solar Queen Series—*Sargasso
of Space*, *Plague Ship*, *Voodoo Planet*, and *Postmarked the Stars*—Dane
Thorson becomes an intergalactic outlaw because of power groups that
constantly strive to limit his freedom. While some may interpret Norton's stance as paranoia or distrust, to do so is to fail to understand her
emphasis. The distrust of the mega-establishments of humanity comes
not from a stress on the groups themselves, rather, it originates in the
value placed on the individual and the dangers that threaten the
individual.

Thus, it is no surprise that all Norton titles feature at least one unusual individual whose uniqueness draws authoritarian attempts at control. Their distinct gifts or talents attract restriction just as surely as innocence draws satanic evil. Even the enlightened and admirable Star Men of *Star Man's Son 2250 A.D.*, Norton's first science fiction novel (which is set in her native Cleveland) distrust the protagonist because he is a mutant. When Fors is refused entry into the Star Men brotherhood of seekers, he must try to fulfill his father's legacy and explore the shattered, wasted world alone. His silver-white hair, extraordinary night sight, and too-keen hearing separate him from his community; however, they also help him achieve goals that no one else can.

The deviations of Norton's characters from social norms make them barely tolerated aliens. Some of this stress may be explained by Norton's isolated childhood and her alienation from her peers. However, a far greater reason is Norton's reverence for the self, especially as it seeks to realize its potentials. This is one of the major reasons why her plots are always so exciting. Her protagonists have to deal not only with dangerous external forces but also with their own maturation and personal challenges. These external and internal processes find their realization through quests in her fiction, and the quests are most frequently set amid cosmic arenas. Intriguingly, at the end of these adventures, protagonists and readers alike are left with only the promises of future successes. For example, Furtig, the mutated cat of *Breed to Come*, must overcome the mythology surrounding his departed human masters if he is to survive their return; and his own self-realization extends far beyond the ending of the novel. In *Android at Arms*, Andas Kastor must discover whether he is an android or a human if he is to save his world, and his rites of passage are just beginning at novel's end.

These quests and rites of passage occur because Norton's characters are creatures of process and action, not ending and resting. Their searches are valuable in and for themselves. Kincar, the main character of *Star Gate*, muses on this active state as his hideous pet and friend Vorken squats on his shoulder:

> Sometimes he thought that an endless quest had been set them for some purpose, and that the seeking, not the finding, was their full reward. And it was good.

In sharp contrast to Norton's compassion for her characters and suspicion of establishments is her raw antagonism toward technology. This may seem odd for one of the twentieth century's major science fiction writers; yet her contempt for science and its products is obvious throughout her works. Aunt Margaret, one of the main characters in the juvenile fantasy *Octagon Magic*, speaks for Norton when she says:

> But in the name of progress more than one crime is committed nowadays. I wonder just who will rejoice when the last blade of grass is buried by concrete, when the last tree is brought down by a bulldozer, when the last wild thing is shot, or poisoned or trapped.

If there is any doubt, Norton is much more emphatic when she speaks directly:

> Yes, I am anti-machine. The more research I do, the more I am convinced that when western civilization turned to machines so heartily with the industrial revolution, they threw away some parts of life which are now missing and which the lack of leads to much of our present frustration.

While Norton's fiction does not fully commit to technophobia and while she distrusts technology more than science, the mechanisms and tools of science are reduced to minor importance in many of her works. This orientation plays a major role in the nature of *Moon of Three Rings*. Long mislabeled as science fiction, it is more correctly a fantasy. Its concern with spaceships and alien planets is only a frame for an adventure based on the transference of human identities and personalities into animal bodies by the power of moon magic. John Rowe Townsend, in *A Sense of Story: Essays on Contemporary Writers for Children*, does an admirable job of describing Norton's use of machines in her works:

> Miss Norton handles her gadgetry with great aplomb. She never draws special attention to it; it is simply there. Spaceships are as ordinary as buses. Flitters for moving around in; stunners and blasters and flamers for dealing with your enemies; and "coms" of all kinds for getting in touch with people are, with countless other devices, casually mentioned in passing without any nudge to the reader.

Thus, the major thrusts of Norton's science fiction must be grouped with those of other such luminaries as Frank Herbert, Ursula K. Le Guin, and Gene Wolfe. They all write what could be variously labeled as "social," "humanistic," or "soft" science fiction. While all their works contain the extrapolated factual material characteristic of science fiction, they really focus on the future of humanity and its possible future traits and societies. Norton comes to this type of writing with a disposition that makes her seek admirable individuals amid future uncertainty (an uncertainty produced in large part by present fascination with technology) and with a triumphant commitment to research that gives her work thorough, but unobtrusive, detail and credibility. In this environment, she produces characters that are, despite their quality, not fully heroic or superhuman, as Frank Herbert's are in *Children of Dune* and *The God-Emperor of Dune*. More realistically, her protagonists have their weaknesses and their foibles. Much of the extreme popularity of her works and much of her successes can be traced to these human creations.

They are souls lost among terrifying forces. As such, they are close enough to readers to encourage empathy and yet special enough to draw admiration. Modern readers can join with the estranged Merlin in *Merlin's Mirror* and sympathize with the circumstances that present us with an unavoidable task that is so isolated that we are left with only a raven as a friend. There is shared revelry in the transformation of Eet in *Uncharted Stars* when we learn that Eet and Murdoc Jern may now consummate their dynamic relationship, which seemed frozen by their differences in shape. Readers may also share in the glory of freedom from prejudice as Kana, in *Star Guard*, fulfills the yet unrealized hope of the twentieth century by his willingness to meet any being as an equal. Just as easily, frustration and sadness may result as Kilda c'Rhyn, in *Dread Companion*, confronts the force of still virulent sexism.

Andre Norton, then, like all special writers, is more than just an author. She is a guide who leads us, the real human beings, to worlds and situations that we might very well expect to live in were we given extraordinary longevity. They are not utopias where all problems have been solved nor are they totally bleak and blighted. Rather, the Norton future is an exciting realm alive with personal quests to be fulfilled and vital challenges to be overcome. Is it any wonder that millions upon millions of readers, spanning three generations, have chosen to go with her in her travels?

Mary T. Brizzi

C. J. CHERRYH AND TOMORROW'S NEW SEX ROLES

In early science fiction, female characters were absent or poorly portrayed. Even women science fiction writers created mostly male protagonists while using females as symbols or archetypes rather than interesting, complex identification-figures. But with the recognition that women read science fiction, and that one appeal of the genre is identification with the main character, writers began to use epic heroines as protagonists.

C. J. Cherryh, however, does something novel. She portrays men who, though they have many virtues of their own, are rather more yielding, who defer to their ladies' judgment, who often must be rescued, who are at times used sexually, and who sometimes even worship the lady. This article explores pairs of epic heroines and helpful males, where the traditional sex roles are reversed. Cherryh is making more than a feminist statement about the potentialities of women raised in the expectation of being strong, courageous leaders. She is also making a statement about the complementary nature of feminine and masculine characteristics, showing that a whole human personality must exhibit both types of qualities. Let us look specifically at Chimele and Aiela in *Hunter of Worlds*, Raen and Jim in *Serpent's Reach*, Melein and Niun in the Faded Sun trilogy, and Morgaine and Vanye in the Morgaine trilogy.

Hunter of Worlds is a densely written study of cultural values, linguistics, and biology. More than an exploration of the Whorf hypothesis that language and thought are interdependent, the novel examines the cultural impact of the ecological role a species may have had before it evolved to sentience. Four sentient species interact in the novel: humanity, amaut, kallia, and iduve. Amaut are a phlegmatic farming race. Kallia are blue, with white hair, possessing a highly evolved social structure where propriety and dignity are paramount. Culturally the most alien group—in spite of their feline beauty with amethyst eyes, indigo skin, and superhuman strength—are the masters of the galaxy, the iduve.

Cherryh, whose field is linguistics, devotes most of her nine-page glossary to the iduve language. So thoroughly does she incorporate the alien tongue into the novel that it is hard to give a plot summary without lengthy, inaccurate explanations of ethical terms. While human, amaut, and kalliran languages are based on subject-predicate structure, the iduve language is based on Tangibles and Ethicals: what is and what it should become. This reflects the evolutionary origin of the iduve: predators. A result in linguistic terms (Cherryh gives many) is that there is no iduve word for *love*. One does not love one's mate, one's family, one's *kameth* or bondsman. The nearest approach to *love* is *m'melakhia*, or desire for acquisition. Since one cannot desire what one already has or what cannot be possessed, loving a bondsman or mate is impossible to the iduve.

The iduve live, not planet-bound, but in huge ships, or *akitomei*, which rove the galaxy bringing civilization and terror to the other three races. Chimele, *orithain* (captain) of the *akites Ashanome*, needs to bring vengeance (rough translation of the iduve *vaikka*) upon her stepbrother Tejef. To help her, she kidnaps a kallia aristocrat, Aiela, to flush Tejef out of his hideout on a human-populated world, Priamos. The relationship between Chimele, an epic heroine, and Aiela, a helpful male, clearly reflects role reversal in this novel.

Chimele, the epic heroine, is placed in a natural leadership role. Aiela, the helpful male, is also a spaceship captain, but early in the novel he is stripped of his kalliran prerogatives and made Chimele's bondsman or *nas-kame*. Even Aiela's name creates the initial expectation of a female character, because it ends in -*a*, which is often a feminine suffix in human languages. Aiela's bondage to Chimele is expressed in terms parallel to a wife's bondage in western civilization. He wears the *idoikkhe*, a jeweled bracelet that communicates commands and punishments. Kings historically bestowed neck, finger, and arm rings upon their thanes to symbolize mutual obligation and privilege. This custom extended to husbands giving ring-pledges to wives to indicate the same set of mutual obligations—the husband to protect and provide, the wife to obey. Chimele establishes such a bond with an arm ring, except that roles are reversed: she commands, while he obeys.

Other characteristics are also reversed with respect to our culture's traditional sex roles. Chimele is physically stronger than Aiela, so much so that the sting of the idoikkhe is a protection of Aiela—she uses a shock to punish him, else her blows might cripple or kill. Chimele, like all iduve, is incapable of weeping; Aiela weeps on many occasions. Chimele is more rational than Aiela. She controls those few emotions she shares with humans—anger, for instance. Softer, more "feminine" emotions she lacks entirely. Her race has no concept of romantic love; Aiela, in contrast, carries pictures of the fiancée he will never see again. Nor do the iduve know the maternal instinct. They do experience a kind of insanity, *dhisais*, during late pregnancy, but only in particular females does this last past childbirth, then manifesting in terrifying ways quite alien to maternal feelings in human mothers. And Chimele, even less than her kin, has little desire to be a mother. Related emotions of sympathy for children and for the weak are absent in the iduve generally and in Chimele specifically. Aiela, in contrast, sympathizes with the attachment of his human ally, Daniel, for a girl whose family has been killed in the siege on Priamos. Chimele, on the other hand, is puzzled by this "weakness" in Daniel and wants him to kill the child to avoid endangering the mission.

Chimele is the dominant one of the pair, assured master over Aiela and her ship. Aiela has also been a ship's captain, but even then his leadership, like that of women in our world, was diluted, subject to consultation with many others. Chimele is incapable of compassion, love, and even hate; she experiences only nuances of pride: *arastiethe* (honor or obligation to exact respect through power), *chanokhia* (elegance), *m'melakhia* (desire to acquire), and especially *vaikka* (revenge). Of these basic iduve emotions, Chimele is most prone to vaikka. To underline the contrast in temperament between Chimele and Aiela, Cherryh never uses Chimele as a point-of-view character. We never know what Chimele is thinking—her emotional strength and control are thus emphasized, a technique Cherryh uses with other epic hero-ines. Aiela, in contrast, is the main point-of-view character. We have frequent insight into his complex relationship with the female kallia, Isande, with whom he is telepathically linked, and into his emotional states. Thus Aiela, whose feelings are more transparent, takes a more traditionally feminine role.

Yet Chimele retains a feminine aura—her beauty and seeming delicacy are emphasized in every physical description. Her skin is "indigo dusted with violet," her eyes "amethyst," her mouth "lavender," her hair, "fine silk." She is "delicate" and "sensuous." Her diction is equally feminine; ironically, she uses words like "indeed," "demented," "perish," "insolent." Her gestures are feminine, almost feline: she dismisses people with a wave of her hand; she touches things "with a violet nail"; she raises her brows ironically; she hisses softly.

Aiela, in contrast, is almost a perfect British gentleman, broad shouldered and slim-hipped, with physical courage surprising even Chimele. His sentences are well framed but direct, his diction less ornate than hers. He uses more imperative sentences; his questions tend to be true requests for information, while Chimele's are sarcasm or grim humor. These techniques build a picture of these two, who reverse traditional role expectations, as biologically male and female.

Other characters also reverse traditional roles—Tejef, for example, is curiously soft and compassionate for an iduve, though he does critically injure his human concubine when she gets maudlin over him. Daniel falls prey to a "motherly" concern for Arle, the refugee child. And Isande at one point refers to herself as "fierce." The novel illuminates the relation of sex roles to culture, evolution, and language. In consequence, it has convincing texture; the reader gets lost in the reality of Cherryh's characters and her world. This, to my mind, reflects her ability to portray both male and female characters, masculine and feminine personality traits. Role reversal contributes to these effects rather than diluting them.

In *Serpent's Reach*, traditional male/female roles are even more clearly reversed. Jim, the helpful male, portrays in mirror image the sexual fantasies writers have traditionally developed about the submissiveness and servility of women.

Among novels of supreme feminine power, *Serpent's Reach* surely tops the list. What more matriarchal life forms are there than ants and bees? The dominant life form of the Hydris planets is the majat, large sentients who live in hives ruled by a Mother, with a social structure similar to ants or bees. When humans come to their home planet, the majat are distressed because the death of a single human is the cessation of an individual consciousness, a situation impossible with their group mind. They finally agree to allow one family, the Kontrins, to live in the system and manage trade relations with the Outside. Horrified by the concept of death to sentient memories, the majat use biochemical expertise to grant immortality to each Kontrin. The protagonist, Raen, is the last scion of the most favored branch of the Kontrins. Raen, an epic heroine, embodies many fantasies of feminine power.

As a Kontrin, Raen is potentially immortal. At the beginning of the novel, her immediate family, the Sul-Meth-maren, is wiped out by dissident Kontrins. Only fifteen years old, she leads a retaliatory raid against her enemies, killing some. This act of derring-do fails, but through the intervention of another powerful and scheming Kontrin female, Moth, Raen inherits the enormous wealth of her family and tours the Hydri system.

Almost a female James Bond, she is an expert at all martial arts; the first time we see her, she is practicing her marksmanship. She is cosmopolitan, sophisticated, even a bit jaded, not just a world traveler, but a planet-hopper. She is backed by a powerful and mysterious agency, the Kontrin clan, though of course many of them are trying to kill her. Like Bond, she is the object of many assassination attempts, which she foils with humor and ease. Like Bond, she is susceptible to the charms of the opposite sex, but unwilling to regard her exploits as anything more than recreation. Some of her partners are enemies, some simply innocent bystanders. Raen is the female mirror-image of the power fantasy represented by James Bond.

But there are no goddesses without mere mortals to lord it over. The Kontrin family have tricked the majat by importing millions of human ova to be raised as servants. These are the beta, mortals living in a capitalistic mercantile society not unlike our own. The betas, in turn, created the azi, sterile slaves who die at age forty. Raen buys and sells azi with casual verbal transactions. The azi are tattooed with identification numbers and trained with Deepstudy for any required task. Though they are used for any unpleasant work, including soldiering (their initiative, not their intelligence, is limited), they generally perform "feminine" tasks: nurturing children, cooking, cleaning, organizing and maintaining a home.

Jim, Raen's helpful male, is an azi. A well-trained entertainer and servant, he is owned by a shipping company and meets Raen as she voyages to Istra. As a male Cinderella figure, he represents the emotional and physical gratifications women generally give to men, except that Jim's and Raen's roles are reversed. Raen acquires Jim in an elaborate and romantic fashion. Bored with the luxury and confinement of interplanetary travel, she decides to gamble with Jim for his "contract." In scenes reminiscent of the casino scenes in James Bond movies, she plays a game called sej with him for his freedom. The power fantasy demands that she win, and of course she does.

The contrast of the two is apparent through their names. *Raen a Sul hant Meth-maren* defines her house (Meth-maren) and clan (Sul). Coined names often imply symbolism: *Meth-* could suggest *Methusalah*, since members of the Kontrin family have lived up to nine hundred years, as did the Biblical patriarch. In *-maren* are overtones of *Mary*, implying the beginning of the New Testament, so the name *Meth-maren* implies the stretch of generations from Genesis to the end of the old order. Indeed, Raen is a harbinger of the new order, for the hives merge, kill each other, and reestablish themselves, as Raen and Moth prophesy. And while Moth (like a hive *Moth*-er) apparently dies, Raen is a bridge, the last Kontrin to survive the hive holocaust. The clan name, Sul, sounds like *sole*, *soul*, or *Sol*. Since sun imagery is so important in Cherryh's work, as in the Faded Sun trilogy and *Downbelow Station*, seeing Raen as a sun-figure makes sense. The sun, prime in the heavens, incorporates all colors, and Raen is recognized by all hives—red, green, gold, and her own blue. So with her given name: Ra is the Egyptian sun-god, and *Raen* also echoes *ray*, a sun ray, and might derive from *Raina*, a form of *Regina*, meaning *queen*, as a hive-queen.

Jim's name is simpler. He has no last name, only a tattooed number to make him unique. Nor is he James; azi pick their own names, and a simple nickname suffices for him. While privileged betas and Kontrins have futuristic names removed from twentieth century America (Pol, Moth, Morn, Delt, Kest, Merek, Paru), the humble azi favor old-fashioned names like Max, Merry, Leo, Sam, or Tim. If he were a James instead of a Jim, it would be interesting that Raen recruits him on a ship, since Christ recruited the apostle James from a fishing boat. Cherryh's epic heroines have a Messianic quality; Raen's Christlike qualities are also reinforced by her "death" after the Ruil raid and "resurrection" after a time underground in the hive.

Many feminist women resent the career advantage men enjoy in the services of a wife who becomes an unpaid servant, domestic, secretary, geisha, and counselor. Jim is a fantasy "wife" to Raen. Upon winning him at the gaming tables, she immediately tries him out in bed. Finding him satisfactory, she then amuses herself by buying him expensive adornments—though a slave, branded by shoulder and eye tattoos, he is an expensively dressed slave, whose affluence speaks well of his owner's prestige. When Raen acquires her new estate, she puts him in charge of the house computer that maintains it. He is condemned through inbred genetic fault to die at forty—but after all, are there any women over forty in James Bond movies? Until then, he is supposed to provide Raen with bedtime companionship.

What goes on in the mind of this wifely paragon? Like the stereotyped repressed female, Jim is awed by Raen. Sex is not important to him, but he craves physical contact. He is terrified that something will happen to this godlike female protector. When she attempts to entertain him with Deepstudy tapes, he tries to memorize them to please her. When she is gone, he winds down like a clockwork doll, catatonic. His training, like that of the traditional super-feminine women, has been directed at making him the perfect slave. Unlike the Stepford wives in a novel of the 1970s, he is even an intelligent slave, one with feelings. You could be sorry for him if his passivity were not so infuriating.

Cherryh does give him one spark of initiative. When Raen leaves to fight evil Kontrins, he sits around wringing his hands until things get out of control. Then he actually disobeys her. She has left certain forbidden tapes, containing sensitive material on Kontrin history. Though previously it has been a big effort for him to overcome his conditioning enough to call her by her first name, he finally audits the tapes and discovers how to protect himself and her from the murderous Pol Hald.

Even in this he is a milksop. Pol Hald himself remarks that all Jim has done is convert himself into a male duplicate of Raen—without her initiative. Jim's reward is to be Raen's immortal companion. She gets the majat, through their chemical expertise, to reverse the genetic sentence of death at age forty. At the end of the book, Raen and Jim are seen as a nouveau Adam and Eve without the Fall, having survived many human generations as an immortal pair. And they are so happy. Why wouldn't they be? Jim is Raen's carbon copy, except submissive.

The Pygmalion story, older than science fiction, is a male fantasy, common enough that it may even please women readers. But when sex roles are reversed, the situation is more thought-provoking. Jim's lack of initiative irritates even feminist readers. The integration does not occur because Jim was never a separate individual. His one act of defiance, auditing the tapes, is insufficient to make him a full person.

In *Serpent's Reach*, all the unpleasant tasks traditionally assigned to females have been transferred to azi, leaving Kontrins and rich betas to playboy freedom. When the hives go through the destructive end of their cycle, however, the rich and powerful are destroyed. Life is restored to those that can both command and serve—run farms, work in fields, bear and raise children. No more azi slaves do the dirty work; no more Kontrin gods make the decisions. Raen gives the message to beta farmers: the slaves will die, never to be replaced. Be independent, have children, and look to the future. Above all, do not enslave yourself or look to masters for salvation. A stratified society of privilege versus slavery will not endure. Only those who can fulfill a variety of roles, both master and servant, both masculine and feminine, will survive in the long run.

Melein, central figure in the Faded Sun trilogy, is the most exalted epic heroine in Cherryh's work. Young, brilliant, gifted with second sight, she leads an entire race, the mri, to salvation. Niun, her brother, follows her in social rank, lacking her vision and knowledge. Sten Duncan, the human who renounces humanity to follow Melein, is another helpful male. At times Melein assumes a Christlike role in *The Faded Sun: Kesrith*, *The Faded Sun: Shon'jir*, and *The Faded Sun: Kutath*.

The mri are mercenary soldiers who at the beginning of *Kesrith* are about to leave the service of the regul, another alien race who have hired them in unsuccessful wars against humanity. Attractive, golden-complexioned humanoids, mri are fierce, proud, and unyielding in war, and secretive about their language and tribal life. The regul, in contrast, are blubbery beings who establish gender only at puberty, about age thirty. Until then, they may be casually killed by a parent or other adult with no sanction. Ethics and imagination are foreign concepts to the regul, but they do have total recall. The regul, having made peace with humankind, cold-bloodedly slaughter all their remaining mri allies, an act of genocide supposedly showing goodwill toward the human victors. Surviving, however, are Melein and Niun, brother and sister, mri priestess (*she'pan*) and warrior (*kel'en*). Given a ship and a human captive, Sten Duncan, they make a journey (*shon'jir*) of over a hundred dead planets to their world of origin, Kutath, where other mri survive. The regul trail them and try to destroy all remaining mri, but ultimately humans save the mri and establish friendship.

Cherryh frequently uses alien civilizations to explore gender-linked role assignment. So with regul and mri. Regul, because they do not know what sex they will be until they reach adulthood and have completed their education, are free of early gender-bound conditioning. Some top regul officials are female. While humans in the abstract are called *man* and referred to as *he*, younglling regul are called *it*, cancelling the sexual bias of language. Amusingly, Cherryh invents the pronoun *degh*, which is appropriate for a being which is potentially male or female, but certainly not neuter, for a regul in the throes of changing to male or female.

This arrangement, however, does not lend itself to sympathetic character development. The regul are at best unimaginative and laughable as the fat, inept younglings trip over each other trying to please adults, whose even greater bulk restricts them to sleds. At worst they are monstrous, as when bai Sharn destroys a beacon meant to signal peace to humans, or when Nagn opens her jaws and narrows her eyes in a predatory smile.

Mri have potential for more sympathetic characters. They have a matriarchal civilization, with a she'pan at the head of each house and of the whole race. Under her are the Sen, scholars who can be either sex; the Kel, warriors also of either sex; and the Kath, children and nurturing women. The whole tribe, therefore, is subordinate to a woman. The she'pan and the Sen, because they are the sole repositories of literacy and learning, make all tribal decisions. Unlike the regul, the matriarchal mri are capable of imagination and vision.

Melein is a superwoman. But Cherryh first allows the reader to absorb the regul prejudice against the mri, considered "bloody-handed savages" incapable of learning, trade, or even subsistence farming. Mri civilization is conservative; the *shon'ai* game and the hal'ari or high language have not changed for 100,000 years. Sheltered in this "backward" culture of mud towers and illiteracy is the fragile, protected Melein. She and Niun even refuse medical aid when she breaks a rib during the regul attack. As the trilogy progresses, however, it becomes apparent that the old she'pan has taught Melein to operate alien spaceships, identify rediscovered dead planets, and successfully command a large mri force under fire. Cannily figuring out that she and Niun have been given a ship so that humans and regul can track them to their planet of origin and destroy them all, she takes her only option, brainwashing Duncan, the human, into becoming her kel'en. Thus he, a human agent, becomes an additional weapon in her hands.

Melein shares another admirable quality with Cherryh's other epic heroines: she is a cool gambler. Arriving on Kutath, the planet from which her tribe has been gone for 100,000 years, she at once challenges a local she'pan. When she'pans challenge, their leading kel'ens fight to the death. The losing she'pan must then die. But Melein takes the chance, and Niun wins, making Melein she'pan in the other's place.

Intelligence, risk-taking, and courage are often qualities ascribed more to males than females. And Melein has another "masculine" quality, her aloofness. The rarity of her moments of honor-giving, touching, or kissing make her more male. All these male qualities are underlined by characteristic technique of never using Melein as point-of-view character. Her thoughts are concealed or inaccurately interpreted through Niun and Duncan.

Niun also reverses traditional sex role assignments. Melein is allowed to read and write, but he is not. Though he is the leader of her Kel, he must ask permission to ask permission to ask a question of her. In *Kesrith*, he has no idea of her plan for mri destiny. The *Pana* is simply an object of worship he has never seen. He has no idea that it contains historical and astrogational data spanning a thousand centuries. Coupled with this naïveté is humility. He is forbidden to think of Melein as his sister. She is the she'pan, ultimate authority. The mri mention gods, but Niun honors Melein more than these abstract deities.

Duncan, the human who turns mri, feels even more humble. When Duncan agrees to turn mri, Niun disposes of all his human property, even medical supplies, and forbids him human language and literacy. Duncan is the burden bearer, not allowed the ritual scars of a true kel'en. The Kutath mri despise him as *tsi*-mri, alien, an abomination. When a mri girl agrees to the custom of spending the night with him, he graciously spares her sexual contact. Duncan's first name is Sten; without stretching symbolism, this suggests the stone or rock in a verse in Matthew. Sten Duncan is humiliated by divided loyalties, but later earns honor in mri lore. Similarly, Peter lies about knowing Christ, but later assumes a key role in Christ's Church.

More convincing evidence of Biblical allusion is found in mri culture. Its representatives live in desert lands and dress in loose robes. Their language sounds Semitic, and mri dialogue has a Biblical cast, flavored with ironic questions. The last *edun*, or dwelling, on Kesrith houses thirteen mri, a fact Cherryh mentions four times; thirteen is the number at the Last Supper. The mri sacred object, the Pana, is like the Ark of the Covenant, but also like the Eucharist. Pana sounds like *panis*, or bread, symbolizing the Eucharist or Body of Christ in the Catholic *Panis Angelicus*. Emergence from the Dark is like resurrection. Triangles and threes are important to mri culture and architecture, perhaps alluding to the Trinity.

Before I explore Melein's Christlike qualities, let me point out other Christlike characters. Intel, the old she'pan, conducts a Last Supper in *Kesrith*. To the thirteen participants, she speaks of her own death and of immortality, as Christ did. They chant the shon'jir (which means "Song of Passings" as well as journey), as those at the Last Supper sang a hymn. Sathell disputes with her and leaves, like Judas. She drinks a cup, though it is different from the Eucharistic cup, being drugged. Meanwhile, Intel and her people are being betrayed, as Christ was, while Stavros, Pilate-like, "kept his hands clean."

Duncan, too, has Christlike qualities. In *Kutath*, we learn his middle initial, X, a cross. His encounters with Sharn, Koch, and Stavros are like Christ's with Pilate. In *Shon'jir*, he is taken to a high place—human ships—and tested, as Christ was, again in Matthew.

But Melein's Messianic qualities are more extensive. Her title, she'pan, includes the root for Pana, holy, forbidden. She'pan implies a female (*she-*) Body of Christ (*pan*). Her surname, *Zain-Abrin*, echoes *Zion* and *Abram*. She wears white robes and often sits with her followers at her feet, as in portraits of Christ. Her ritual scars resemble stigmata. She comes to bring "not peace, but a sword," but actually both, since the ship *Flower* is carrying peaceful scientists, and *Sabre* is carrying a military force. Her ship, *Fox*, reminds us of the passage: "The foxes have holes . . . but the Son of Man hath not where to lay his head," especially when the Kutath she'pan challenges her to establish a House. The ship *Santiago* suggests the apostle Saint James, but in the Spanish form, *Iago*, suggesting treachery.

As she'pan, death is taboo to her, as Christ overcame death. Her weeping when she recovers the Pana, with Duncan and Niun waiting, following Intel's "Last Supper" and before her capture has overtones of Gethsemane. Wounded in the side, as Christ was pierced after crucifixion, she lies in a coma, as if dead. When "resurrected," she puts on white robes and becomes leader of all mri. From Duncan she demands, as Christ demanded of his disciples, that he leave everything to follow her. On Kutath, she is accused of consorting with tsi-mri, aliens, as Christ was accused of consorting with publicans and sinners. But before the instruments of Ah'ehon, she is transfigured in light. One speech especially reflects her Messianic qualities:

> "I am the foretold," Melein said, "And I call on you for your children and their strength, for the purpose for which we went out in the beginning, and I shall build you a House, she'panei."

Though the strongest of Cherryh's epic heroines, Melein does not overshadow Niun and Duncan. They, too, have strength and ingenuity, strong Hands, though she is Head. Melein has been a member of all three castes, Kath, Kel, and Sen. She encompasses and contains all. But the structure of mri society emphasizes the need for different qualities—"male" and "female"—for a superior personality like Melein's. Divinity itself is not all male, but partakes of the feminine as well. It takes Head, Hand, and Heart to make a whole being.

The medieval romance background of the Morgaine trilogy, *Gate of Ivrel*, *Well of Shiuan*, and *Fires of Azeroth*, is suggested in the earth, air, water, and fire in the titles. Cherryh's epic heroine in the trilogy is Morgaine, and her helpful male is Vanye.

Morgaine, from a civilization more technologically advanced than ours, is one of a dedicated cadre sent forth to destroy the dangerous Gates of Power, which were discovered by a humanoid race called (variously) khal, qujal, or qhal. These Gates, among other powers, permit not just instantaneous interstellar travel, but also time travel, so that qhal civilization has spread throughout the galaxy and into future time. Since some qhal travelers have attempted to travel backward in time, paradoxes have occurred, destroying whole worlds. Morgaine is the last survivor sent forward to explore the Gate network and close each Gate as she passes through. Her companions have all perished. Since there is no return, Morgaine is on a suicide mission.

In her travels, she picks up an *ilin*, or hearth-thane, bound to her service for a year. This is Vanye, a disgraced son. The two fight their way into the master Gate in Ivrel, but a qhal manages to get through the Gate with them. This qhal (call him Zri-Liell for the moment) is a nasty sort, having used Gate power to transfer his mind from an aging body to the strong young body of Roh, Vanye's cousin and only true friend. Vanye swears to kill Zri-Liell. The attempt to destroy the Gates in Shiuan and Azeroth, with the vengeance quest against Zri-Liell-Roh, motivate the action of the second two books.

Morgaine's heroism is of character, not supernormal powers. Like Melein, she has superior technical knowledge and carries with her a laser gun, antibiotics, and Changeling, a sword which utilizes Gate power to throw things in its field into a distant space-time. She is also quick of apprehension, brave in battle, dedicated, a good horsewoman, and a canny bargainer. Strikingly beautiful, with white hair, tall as a man of Vanye's world, she has alien, perhaps qhalish, blood. She exhibits feminine charm and humor in her fastidious roasting of game, which contrasts amusingly to the studied masculine poses she assumes before her enemies, and her courteous suggestion that Vanye be not "overnice" in sharing her bed reflects cozy companionability. Her quaint substitution of the pronoun *thee* for *you* gives her an elegance of speech. Quixotic charm, determination, and quick-witted skill are her main attributes.

Like sword-and-sorcery, the trilogy draws on medieval romance, particularly the Grail legend—but in an inverted way. Morgaine and Vanye are knight and squire, *liyo* and ilin, *arrhen* and *khemeis*, king and thane, Don Quixote and Sancho Panza, but the twist is that the knight or king figure is Morgaine, female. Like King Arthur, she wields a magic sword. Arthur's surname is Pendragon; her sword's handle is formed like a dragon. Like Gawain, whose name hers echoes, she is on a quest to save the land. She passes through Waste Lands (though Shiuan is drowning, not arid, the lands around the Gates are infertile and dying much like those in the Gawain legends). Kasedre resembles the sick Fisher King. She has healing powers, from her first-aid kit, as Gawain had healing herbs.

Her name seems feminine in origin: Morgan le Fay. But she more resembles Merlin. Like him, she has been imprisoned in a rock (one of the Gates), and like him, she shapes history, disappearing and reappearing after years of being only legend. Like Merlin, she is a worker of good, unlike Morgan le Fay, who was evil.

Vanye has qualities traditionally assigned to women. Illegitimate child of a woman dead in childbirth, he has been raised where he is considered second best. He strives to earn adult privileges, but when, in late adolescence, he slays his brother in self-defense, he is cast out by his father when he refuses to save his honor by killing himself.

Branded a coward, he is set out with no means of livelihood and finally taken up by Morgaine. Like an unwanted female child in a male-oriented world, he turns to a protector—not a husband, but a female.

Morgaine claims Vanye as ilin by slashing his hand and tasting his blood—a parody of the blood-show of a virginal wedding night. She smears her hearth-ash into the wound, reminder of household duties. He is then bound to obey her, and she is bound to provide for him, though she may mistreat him in other ways. Their role reversal is symbolized in *Azeroth* by her riding a stallion and him riding a mare.

Even as sex roles are interchanged, there are other types of role reversal. Through most of the books, Vanye regards Morgaine as mad. When, in *Ivrel*, she rides in terror from him, suspecting his body to be inhabited by Zri-Liell, he sees this as madness, which to the reader seems only good sense. Her whole quest, to Vanye, is madness. This inversion also occurs with the barrows-girl Jhirun, who, condemned to a life of drudgery as the wife of her brutal cousin Fwar, slashes his face and runs away after a ghostly barrows-king. But, Jhirun wryly ruminates, it is they who are mad, eking out existence in the face of slow death, while she, in trying to escape, is alone sane among them.

Another inversion involves the attitude toward good and evil. Morgaine is really a public-spirited heroine, devoted to saving a whole universe from the disasters of time paradox from the Gates. But everywhere, legends of Morgaine depict her as an evil witch. In Ivrel, she has lost 10,000 soldiers because they would not obey her order to retreat. But legend says she lured them to destruction. Vanye sees her as a beautiful poisonous snake gliding among lesser beings. In Shiuan, she is known as Morgen-Angharen—spirit of death. Her emblem, a seagull feather, is hung at windows to ward off the dead.

The qhal suffer similar bad press, with more justice. In Ivrel, they are body snatchers, creators of monsters. In Shiuan, they are effete, decadent lords. In Azeroth, however, we see their potential for good— Merir and his court, like good fairies or the Round Table, protect humankind and tend the forest like a garden. At the end, Shathon is left in the hands of peaceful qhal and humans who pair like Ellur and Sin, qhal and human, knight and squire. The whole movement of the trilogy is from opposing dualities, good and evil, male and female, mad and sane, qual and human, showing that blending or pairing of opposites will result in the best outcome.

Resolution of dualities in Roh is more complex, since even Vanye does not know at times Roh's identity. Though Zri-Liell has snatched Ron's body through Gate-power, some personality characteristics of the good Roh remain with the possessed body. Every time Vanye encounters Roh-Zri-Liell, the good qualities become more pronounced. When we first meet Zri-Liell, he has slashed throats and plots seduction or rape in a stolen body. But later he becomes remorseful and finally tries to create an alliance with Morgaine and Vanye. At the end of *Azeroth*, he defends these two in battle and resists the temptation of the Gate, spending his last days in service as squire. This shift of sympathies is accomplished by resolution of dualities, and Cherryh creates a truly sympathetic character by blending opposites.

This reconciliation of opposites also occurs in Vanye. At the beginning, Vanye's father hacks off Vanye's hair to show loss of honor. Further humiliation comes with Vanye's service to Morgaine. But at the end of the trilogy, Morgaine helps him braid up the grown-out hair again, restoring honor, and this intimate service makes them more than kin, resolved polarities, male and female in transcendent partnership:

> "Never," she said, "have I power to listen to heart more than head. Thee's my better nature, Vanye. All that I am not, thee is. . . . And thee will do what thee thinks right; and so must I, thee by heart, I by head."

It is not strange to see masculine and feminine components as both needed in a rounded personality—what is unusual is Cherryh's vision of "head" being the female component, while "heart" is the male.

Vivid characterization, indeed the sheer variety and number of characters in each novel, are a keystone to Cherryh's success. And basic to this success is her unconventional treatment of male and female personality traits. Her epic heroines are unswerving, rational, godly, dominant; her helpful males are confused, faulted, submissive, and emotional, opposite to traditional roles. She challenges male and female stereotypes, drawing compellingly original and convincing portraits. Role-reversed pairs make a statement about the complementary nature of "feminine" and "masculine" traits, suggesting that a whole personality must partake of both qualities. A symbol of this type of personal integration occurs in *Wave without a Shore*, with the ahnit statue of two lovers, which seems to lack a third figure—but, as Sbi explains, the third figure, the lover's child, is the viewer himself or herself, who creates his or her own identity and reality out of the polarities of male and female in his or her culture. What appears, in Cherryh's books with epic heroines, to be superficially a feminist statement about the heroic possibilities of females and the helping possibilities of males is actually a more profound, but still feminist, statement about the creative androgyny of the human spirit.

5

Adam J. Frisch

TOWARD NEW
SEXUAL IDENTITIES:
JAMES TIPTREE, JR.

For those who myth from fact would know
Dwell not in the Quintana Roo.

The Quintana Roo, a primitive area in the eastern Mexican Yucatan, serves as the setting for several of the short stories by science fiction writer James Tiptree, Jr. A stark, empty land sparsely inhabited by ancient Mayan peoples, the Quintana Roo provides a sharp contrast to modern western civilization; it suggests the vast, unorganized turbulence lying beneath our twentieth century's technological identity. Thus, it provides an excellent landscape from which Tiptree can explore her central concern as a science fiction writer: the psychological consequences of the war between contemporary logical thought and primitive mythical thought and between the patterns of science and the patterns of fiction, which characterize the modern human condition.

James Tiptree, Jr., whose real name is Alice Hastings Sheldon, was born near Chicago, Illinois, in 1916. The daughter of naturalist Herbert Bradley and mystery writer Mary Hastings, Tiptree as a child often accompanied her parents on wildlife expeditions to Africa and Indonesia, trips that may have sparked her later interest in the study of behavioral psychology. Tiptree did not begin publishing science fiction until she was fifty-two, the year after she completed a Ph.D. degree in psychology from George Washington University. From 1968, the time of her first publication, to 1977, Tiptree's real identity remained unknown. Then an interview in the science fiction publication *Locus* revealed that she was an experimental psychologist living in Virginia, the wife of Dr. Huntington Denton Sheldon and the mother of two children. During her career Tiptree has concentrated on science fiction short stories and novellas, which, through 1981, have won three Hugo and four Nebula awards. Her one novel, *Up the Walls of the World*, was published in 1978. Almost all of Tiptree's science fiction writing is influenced by her observation of human behavioral motivations; it is the study of psychology that forms for her the link between science and fiction.

Perhaps the most dominant theme in Tiptree's works is the psychological pain and the lack of personal fulfillment human beings experience when they allow themselves to remain isolated in limited patterns of behavior. Tiptree's fiction particularly focuses upon two such behavioral models, one of which has historically been associated with "male" conduct and the other of which has traditionally been labeled as typically "female" behavior. Tiptree identifies the male behavior pattern as involving psychological drives for survival and for order in the environment, goals customarily linked with "unemotional" systems of logical thought. Conversely, her stereotypical female figure is the overly protective, loving mother, actively concerned about the welfare of others but always passive about her own well-being. For Tiptree, an exclusive preoccupation with either of these traditional sexual models will lead not only to a severe retardation of an individual's development but also to pain, stagnation, and possibly death for members of that individual's society.

The three male astronauts in Tiptree's story "Houston, Houston, Do You Read?" offer excellent illustrations of the dangers of an overly masculine orientation. The astronauts have been on a circumsolar space mission when their capsule was caught in a gigantic solar flare and hurled forward in time. They emerge into a world where Earth's only inhabitants are cloned females, the other half of the population having been destroyed by a global plague. The spacemen are rescued from their cramped capsule, which lacks sufficient fuel for a return to Earth, by the female crew of the spacious, ecologically self-sufficient explorer ship *Gloria*. But the women discover that even a year-long journey back to Earth is not adequate time to wean the males away from the patriarchal patterns of thought that constitute their only meaning in life. Engineer Bud Geirr, driven by severe penis anxieties, pursues the women aboard *Gloria* to the point of an attempted rape. Commander Norman Davis displaces his sexual drives into a religious authoritarianism that eventually causes him to attempt a takeover of the rescue craft. And even the story's likable and well-meaning narrator, ship scientist Doc Lorimer, cannot escape behavioral anxieties stemming from a traumatic childhood incident in a girl's lavatory, which force him continually to prove to himself that "I'm not a girl. I'm a boy." The women aboard *Gloria* conclude that, while male aggressiveness may once have been necessary to "save society from the crazies," it now has little to contribute to their civilization. The male astronauts find themselves, like the character Bustamente in another Tiptree story, "the primordial Big Man who organized the race and for whom the race has so little more use." In a world where "what males protect people from is largely other males," masculinity in the historical sense can only be considered a "disease," and the women aboard *Gloria* eventually administer to the astronauts what they consider the only possible "antidote."

An even more extreme vision of the coldness and aggressiveness that Tiptree associates with the male behavior stereotype is presented in the short story descriptively entitled: "The Psychologist Who Wouldn't Do Awful Things to Rats." Tilly Lipsitz, an experimental psychologist like Tiptree herself, is constantly humiliated by his colleagues and department head because he believes too strongly in the organic unity of life to dissect his specimens with "proper" scientific detachment. Lipsitz instead tries to keep his cages clean and well aired, often ruining many of his experiments by impulsively feeding his animals extra treats. Threatened eventually with the loss of his grant, Lipsitz gets drunk one evening and returns to the laboratory to destroy his specimens and start anew. Once there, however, Lipsitz fantasizes a confrontation between adherents to the "unreal" community of all living things, led by the legendary Rat King, and members of the "real" world whose competitiveness and emotional coldness have spawned both industrial progress and the horrors of an Auschwitz. Regrettably for Lipsitz, he chooses the latter world vision, and the story's final pages show the consequential beginnings of intellectual and emotional deteriorations based upon his choice.

But although Tiptree rejects the historical role of the male as an aggressive patriarch, she also cautions against an exclusive acceptance of traditionally female behavior patterns such as intellectual noncompetitiveness or personal passivity. Tiptree believes that excessive emphasis on either sexual stereotype will retard the development of both the individual and his or her society. If males have been history's "guerillas," then women have been the "opossums . . . living in a toothless world," according to Ruth Parsons in the story "The Women Men Don't See." This work, narrated by hunter-fisherman Don Fenton, tells the story of a quartet marooned in the Quintana Roo by an airplane crash. As Don Fenton and Ruth Parsons hike through the wilderness seeking fresh water or human aid, Ruth gradually reveals the extent of her alienation from and sexual frustration with the twentieth-century, male-dominated world. "Men," claims Ruth, "live to struggle against each other; we're just part of the battlefield. It'll never change unless you change the whole world." The problem with maintaining this attitude, as Ruth discovers, is that it tends toward self-fulfillment, as its adherent becomes a passive survivor whose responses further reinforce the very alienation originally causing the problems. Indeed, so "alien" does Ruth become to Don that at a critical moment he wounds her rather than one of the extraterrestrial beings who have discovered the pair. Ruth Parsons escapes her victimization by some shrewd bargaining that secures for her and her pregnant daughter passage off Earth aboard the alien vessel, but this option hardly seems viable—even symbolically—to her fellow victims of twentieth-century masculine mistreatment. In fact the main female character in another Tiptree story, "The Screwfly Solution," when facing a similar victimization ends up committing suicide. Although Tiptree may ultimately be more sympathetic toward female passivity than toward male aggressiveness, she never endorses the "opossum" approach to life advocated by women characters such as Ruth Parsons.

Tiptree rejects all unibehavioral attitudes toward life because for her they invariably lead both the individual and his or her community to that form of psychological stagnation known as narcissism or selfishness. For example, even while exposing the dominant-submissive behavioral problems of the three male astronauts in "Houston, Houston," Tiptree is careful to suggest the flaws in the all-female society that finally condemns them. This female-dominated Earth has become atrophic and overly reflexive, as symbolized both by its population decline to only eleven thousand clone types and by the paucity of its new creations (all termed "Woolagongs" after its sole "inventor" clone type). Another short story, "Her Smoke Rose Up Forever," even more clearly demonstrates the dangers inherent in any "me only" approach to life. Peter, the story's narrator, discovers through a series of painful flashbacks that he has always been so concerned with his own personal tragedies that he has never truly loved another person. Whether searching for the very best duck blind as a boy or seeking a prize-winning formula as a professional scientist, Peter finds that this powerful selfishness has changed each moment of possible life triumph into a bitter-tasting personal defeat, until at last his personality has become locked into an alien-invoked energy pattern in an eternity he most desperately longs to escape. Clearly, Tiptree insists upon the elemental need for getting beyond one's singular self.

Yet, somewhat paradoxically, Tiptree condemns the complete abandonment of that self. Her stories emphasize that it is the very incompleteness of the individual, his or her "haploid" condition, that produces human creative vitality. Just as Freud identified the pulse of life as originating from the irreconcilable struggle between order-loving ego and death-desiring id, so Tiptree sees our traditional male/female role divergences as symbolic of the life/death dialectic whose potential sparks all that we find meaningful in existence. Thus, Tiptree's fiction continually warns the reader away from any reductionistic solution that would destroy human potential simply by abandoning self-concern.

For example, Tiptree's short story "She Waits for All Men Born" depicts the final, fatal merging of the life and death forces that have powered human evolution from its beginning. Snow, a blind but immortal mutant girl with pale-white eyes, is born into a postholocaustic world where a slowly diminishing band of civilized humans battles a growing number of cannibalistic fliers who seek children for food. Like the first Pelicosaur pup, who is shown early in the story acquiring an instinct for "action under stress," Snow automatically reacts when threatened by telepathically destroying the danger with her blank, silver gaze. But since all living beings, whether friends or enemies, inherently pose a potential danger to her immortality, Snow finds herself eventually destroying all life within her immediate vicinity, until she finally becomes "the last human . . . wandering and waiting alone through the slow centuries for whatever may come from the skies." Through this figure of the eternal child, Tiptree warns the reader of the cold, lonely stasis that will result should humanity ever learn to reconcile its life-oriented and death-oriented impulses.

Tiptree illustrates this same theme on a cosmic scale in the novella "A Momentary Taste of Being." Aaron Kaye is the doctor aboard the explorer ship *Centaur*, which is desperately searching for other habitable planets for overpopulated humanity. Aaron's sister Lory returns alone from her scouting team carrying on her tiny ship a bioluminescent creature discovered on an Edenic planet circling Alpha Centauri. Certain discrepancies in her story and a strange illness breaking out aboard *Centaur*, however, cause the alien creature to be kept under quarantine until Aaron's sister can be more closely examined. Eventually, because of the population pressures back home as much as for logical reasons, the decision is reached to lift the quarantine and colonize the planet. But when the alien on Lory's ship is freed, it mesmerizes the entire *Centaur* crew with brilliant pulsating colors, sending each member into a transcendent but fatal coma. Aaron Kaye alone is left alive to speculate that humanity itself may simply have been the male "sperm cells" of some giant cosmic force seeking union with the female "eggs" of the Centauri system. Lory had labeled the man-alien merger "the end of pain," but Aaron Kaye recognizes that through this blending, humanity will lose its individual distinctiveness and hence its existence as one of life's contributing species.

Tiptree is also uncomfortable with that blend of male and female personalities known as the "androgyne," a figure most popular in modern feminist writings. Her 1981 short story "Lirios," for example, depicts the seduction of a young American beach drifter in the Quintana Roo by an androgynous, buccaneerlike manifestation of the sea. Because the young American believes that the impersonal sea will "give you anything you need," he regards the apparition he finds one midnight tied to the spar of an ancient ship as both powerfully aggressive and sexually irresistible. The local Mayans, however, consider such a figure demonic rather than holy. They believe such spirits rob one of his soul, and they call the spot where these spirits appear "El Paso del Muertes," the place of the dead. The young American ignores their cautions and disappears to seek out his androgynous apparition, but the story's narrator is left feeling much more ambivalent about this "life-hungry succubus . . . seductive as a ruby, more terrible than all the petty armies of man . . . [whose] life is ours."

If exclusive adherence to male or female behavior patterns is considered by Tiptree to be inevitably destructive and if she also believes that their distinctness is crucial to vitality in a species, what sort of behavioral ideal does Tiptree favor? How should the individual who wishes to develop physically, morally, and aesthetically proceed? Tiptree's answer seems to lie in a kind of pluralistic union of human sexual patterns. She favors a psychological synthesis in which both sexes retain their behavioral identities while simultaneously learn to appreciate and incorporate selectively the most important goals and attitudes of their sexual counterparts. Tiptree is not advocating some kind of bland, best-of-both-worlds abstraction; rather, she is seeking to delineate the kind of individuals who can be comfortable with their own sexual identities yet who can call upon the power arising from their own incompleteness to develop even in times of crisis. Perhaps the best illustrations of Tiptree's pluralistic ideal appear as the main characters in her longest work, the 1978 novel *Up the Walls of the World*.

Tiptree's novel takes place in three distinct locales. The first and most imaginative of these settings is the wind-swept planet Tyree, whose telepathic inhabitants live amid the turbulences of their world's upper atmosphere. Tiptree gives this race of flying beings a highly developed sense of individual "aura," so that their physical identities manifest themselves in pulsating energy fields that expand or contract at will. The Tyrenni regard the privacy of each individual's energy field as sacrosanct and have created the concept of *ahura* to denote their ideal combination of "mind-privacy-smoothness." Any attempt at mind fusion is regarded by the Tyrenni as the worst of crimes. Tiptree also gives the Tyrenni a highly developed aesthetic sense, appropriate to creatures who must be sensitive to the slightest wind variation, and this keen perception leads to many synesthetic reversals of human sensory experience. For example, the Tyrenni perceive all light as sound, and all emotions as combinations of colors and sounds, so that their sun is called "the Sound" and fear is always manifested as "a green squeal." Even the sexual act itself is reversed by Tiptree. Intercourse on Tyree involves a pair's achieving the utmost distance from each other while still maintaining contact, as opposed to our human desire for a close embrace. All these reversals spill over into behavioral modes, which was the primary reason Tiptree created them. For example, the women on Tyree are "naturally" considered their race's explorers and providers, whereas the males are physically dominant enough to be "capable" of controlling and educating the children. Thus, the main Tyrenni character, the young lady Tivonel, considers her desires for freedom and adventure intrinsically feminine traits: "I love my female life," she thinks at one point, ". . . travel, work, exploration, trade, the spice of danger." Conversely, Tivonel feels somewhat guilty about her "masculine" impulses to cherish her child or to pursue "domestic" tasks, such as logical speculative thought, although she finds silly the arguments of the radical Paradomin sect of Tyree females that claim that if women were allowed the strengthening task of child-raising they would hold the power in society. Tivonel's beloved, Giadoc, similarly combines a Tyrenni male mind of scientific discipline with a "motherly" desire for adventure and travel. Even as such mixtures of human behavioral norms encourage the reader to posit alternative possibilities for his or her own twentieth-century culture, they propel Tivonel and Giadoc into the only possible survival responses when crisis faces their planet.

A second set of chapters in Tiptree's novel takes place on present-day Earth, where Dr. Daniel Dann is providing cursory medical service to a small group of psychological "misfits" involved in an extrasensory perception project. When this group begins to achieve documentable telepathic success, Earth's "male" military minds move in—complete with their black Labradors—to exploit the group's powers for themselves. But rather than dwell on the destructiveness of the military mind set, Tiptree uses it as a foil to set off the more flexible mentalities of her main human characters. Dr. Dann, driven to drug addiction by a past failure to be "masculine" enough to rescue family members from a burning building, at first considers himself a complete failure as a human being since his only asset seems to be the rather worthless ability to sympathize with his patients' pain and isolation. He longs for the scientific detachment to regard others as numbers rather than as persons, as his fellow doctors can. It is not until Dr. Dann can accept himself as both a powerful person and a sympathetic human being that he comes to understand the link between the pain of isolation and the joy of love. His is the universal personal predicament, as one of the poems he quotes to himself suggests: "What else, when chaos turns all forces inward to shape a single leaf?" Like many of his "misfit" patients, Dann eventually finds his apparent emotional liability a survival factor when cosmic rather than terrestrial perspectives become involved. A similar reversal also happens to the main female character on Earth, the computer analyst Margaret Omnali, who at the novel's start has retreated to the unemotional coldness of logic circuitry following a childhood sexual trauma. It is precisely her mixture of paternal logic and matriarchal protectiveness that eventually allows Omnali to assume control of a gigantic alien gas cloud apparently threatening both Earth and Tyree.

The third group of chapters is set within the huge gas cloud itself. And it is here that Tiptree most fundamentally posits the need for all life forms to maintain their pluralistic behavioral structures. The Destroyer, as the cloud is named by the Tyrenni, has a primitive form of self-consciousness that allows it to drift apart from synchrony with others of its kind. Feeling a profound guilt at this separation, the giant being searches through space, seeking a logical alternative to the task for which it feels it was formed but destroying whole worlds in the process. Eventually, its duty/guilt "intolerable stress" and its inherent "great contradiction of underlying realities" compels it to make itself vulnerable to the spirit of Margaret Omnali. She teaches it in turn never to allow the potential gradient of energy known as life to "fall to zero," and she eventually finds it a task worthy of its immense powers.

Tiptree's novel *Up the Walls of the World* is significant not only because it delineates thematically and individually the author's beliefs about the necessity for behavioral mixes but also because its use of stylistic devices such as synesthesia and multiple points of view forces readers to create within their own minds the kinds of psychological syntheses the book's own themes endorse. As a prelude to examining the ways in which Tiptree achieves these effects, let us first consider the following imagistic description:

> We emerge dry-mouthed into a vast windy salmon sunrise. A diamond chip of sun breaks out of the sea and promptly submerges in cloud.

This colorful passage, which might be picturing the windy world of Tyree but in fact is describing a sunrise over the Quintana Roo in "The Women Men Don't See," does a precise job of externalizing the fragmented emotional feelings of its narrator, Don Fenton. The description is torn between images of sterility (such as "dry-mouthed," "windy" and "chip of sun") and images associated with wetness and fecundity (such as "salmon," "sea," and "cloud"). The passage polarizes vastness ("vast windy . . . sunrise") with sharp delineation ("diamond chip"), an opening upward movement ("We emerge . . .") with a descending closure phrase (". . . promptly submerges in cloud"). These internal tensions within the short description mirror the internal strife Fenton feels as he suddenly finds himself isolated in a wilderness and alienated from his sole female companion.

It is not an exaggeration to claim that the majority of Tiptree's descriptions depend for their effect on a similar kind of internal polarization of imagery. Often this contrast is prominently displayed. In "Her Smoke Rises Up Forever," Peter's recollections of the various events in his life are punctured by sudden flashes of "black!—light!—black!" caused (unknown to him) by conditions external to his visions but incorporated by Peter into the imagery of his dreams (e.g., "the black path in the silver lake" and "the moon jumps out of a black sky like a locomotive headlight"). A similar black-versus-white dichotomy permeates the award-winning story, "Love Is the Plan, the Plan Is Death," in which a male alien creature confronts his own and his race's aggressive impulses while he searches for his destined mate. Tiptree will also employ other color contrasts. For example, the boy Timor in "The Milk of Paradise" is continually torn between the pale pinkness of his human ancestry and the drab grayness of the beings he has come to admire on the planet Paradise, a conflict highlighted by the emotional coldness of the pink world as opposed to the tender warmth of the gray. But whether Tiptree employs a prominent color contrast or a more subtle internal polarization of imagery, her descriptions serve to externalize the tensions every individual faces by virtue of his or her incompleteness. Some characters, such as Peter in "Her Smoke Rises Up Forever," never manage to resolve that incompleteness and hence remain trapped in their "black-and-white" worlds forever. Others mistakenly select one pole of the dialectic only, such as Timor in "The Milk of Paradise," who opts for the gray world of total love but in the process gives up his inheritance as a civilized human being. But the truly successful characters manage to attain a plurality of color in their world visions. When Margaret Omnali in *Up the Walls of the World*, for example, obtains her first sight of the cosmos from within the alien cloud, Tiptree tells us: "Her mind which had always flinched from the hot closeness of human color [was] enchanted with this infinity of spectral fires."

Tiptree will often choose what seems like an insignificant place name or detail for a story title precisely because its image synthesizes the larger contradictions underlying the story itself. For example, the Quintana Roo story "Lirios" is named after an abandoned Yucatan resort ("The Lilies"), which receives only occasional mention as the locale of the young American's encounter with the sea spirit. But those few observations carefully establish that the resort failed because of a "rotten back-flow" offshore that proved fatal to several of its guests, just as the area's back-flows in culture and in time apparently overcome the young beach wanderer. Tiptree sets several of her stories in the Quintana Roo because this "world's biggest absolutely flat green-grey rug" provides a perfect liminal landscape between civilization and its primitive roots. Like the Jurassic lizards and ancient Mayans native to this land, Tiptree's characters find during each trek into the Quintana Roo that they become "soaked in slime . . . desiccated . . . smelling like the Old Cretaceous." In a similar manner, the novel *Up the Walls of the World* is named after a locale on Tyree whose eternal mixture of upwellings and down drafts represents that "dense dying with life," which is the novel's central tension. This location near one of Tyree's "poles" is called the Wall of the World (singular), but it symbolizes all the walls (plural) that separate life from life, sexual pole from sexual pole, and planet from planet in our cosmos.

Tiptree's frequent use of multiple points of view also draws readers into the role of synthesizer as they attempt to fit the plot together. The sectional shifts between the worlds of Tyree, Earth, and the alien gas cloud, for instance, are frequently marked by repetitive vocabulary transitions that encourage readers to link the separate visions. Chapter 2, for example, which is set on Tyree, ends with the words: "She is Tivonel, merry creature of the Great Winds of Tyree, on her life way." Chapter 3, which takes place on Earth, begins with the sentence: "Doctor Daniel Dann is on his life way too." Much power is released by the simple connective "too," for it forces the reader to adopt a distanced, omniscient viewpoint capable of accommodating both worlds' visions. Similar transitions dot other parts of this novel: for example, in Chapters 21 and 22, Omnali and the gas cloud both end their meditations with the phrase: "I must follow, I must search . . ." Sometimes Tiptree's works shift location in time through complicated series of flashbacks, sometimes they shift spatial points of view, and sometimes they sweep through evolutionary time spans and cosmic distances simultaneously. But whatever her particular technique, seldom does Tiptree allow readers merely to observe passively; we must forge philosophical and behavioral unions for ourselves.

The job of science fiction authors is a difficult one, for the very nature of this genre forces them to unite the power that lies in scientific truth with the emotional wisdom that abides in a fictional vision. By using the insights of psychology, which combine the penetrating accuracy of science with the archetypal significances of myth, James Tiptree, Jr., continues to form imaginative creations that show us who we are as modern, sexual, and human beings.

Marleen Barr

HOLDING FAST TO FEMINISM AND MOVING BEYOND: Suzy McKee Charnas's The Vampire Tapestry

Suzy McKee Charnas describes her first novel, *Walk to the End of the World* (1974), as "a story of a society in which power is the crucial question, and the struggle between generations of males is the central form that question takes, while mothers and daughters figure only as labor, brood mares, and objects of aggression. The book ended up being about sexism carried to a logical extreme, and it suggests, I hope, the inherent destructiveness of any society in which one portion of the population enslaves and dehumanizes another." The "society" Charnas speaks of is called the Holdfast. It is a postholocaust community where nonwhite "evil races," and even animals, no longer exist after the "wasting of the world"—four-legged animals, that is. In *Walk*, "man" and "beast" are synonomous. Some Holdfast men run in packs of "Rovers"; all Holdfast women spend their first years scrounging for food on the floor of the "kit-pen." Throughout their lives, these women are reduced to a subhuman level. They are the slaves of men and are called "fems." The fem Alldera, who is not introduced until the novel's sixty-sixth page, is its heroine. The portrayal of man's inhumanity to man—and especially to women—forms the crux of her story.

Alldera is also at the center of *Motherlines* (1978), a novel about a matriarchal society of proud and free "Riding Women." When contemplating this sequel to *Walk*, Charnas wondered, "To begin with, who would publish a science fiction book only about women? . . . I meant to write a book about women who were neither victims nor monsters. And if I succeeded, would more than a handful of women . . . ever read it?" Her comment points to the book's main concern: feminism. And, like *Walk*, it also addresses the question of the relationship between man and beast. The Riding Women are, of course, quite dependent upon horses. What is not initially clear, however, is the extent of their dependency; Riding Women cannot reproduce without the presence of stallions. Alldera learns to accept this as well as other aspects characterizing life among the Riding Women of the Motherline Tribes. The novel explains how she, and fellow "free-fems," acquire a sense of purpose and dignity in a world of women located just beyond the boundaries of the patriarchal and pathological— Holdfast.

In *The Vampire Tapestry* (1980), which has been called "possibly the outstanding vampire novel of all time," man and beast are present in the person of Dr. Edward Lewis Weyland, a distinguished professor who just happens to be a vampire. He can conveniently study and feed upon human subjects at his Cayslin College dream research center. This practical arrangement ends when, after his nonhuman traits are discovered, he is forced to leave Cayslin. The novel describes the vampire's adventures as he tries to survive in Manhattan and Santa Fe. He undergoes psychoanalytic therapy, is caged by a villain, and commits murder. Each chapter can stand alone, and two appeared separately in *Omni* and *New Dimensions II*. Chapter Three, "Unicorn Tapestry," won the Nebula Award for the Best Novella of 1980. Like Charnas's first two novels, *Vampire* also questions the traditions of popular literature. Science fiction writer Elizabeth A. Lynn explains: Charnas takes "that whole traditional structure of vampires and turn[s] it inside out and [does] what she wants with it and [she makes] a nice gloss on civilized structures at the same time. I really enjoyed that."

Feminist readers of Suzy McKee Charnas's *Walk to the End of the World* and *Motherlines* might feel disgruntled by the publication of *The Vampire Tapestry*. The novel is not the promised and expected completion to the *Walk/Motherlines* trilogy. Those who were looking forward to seeing Alldera triumphantly leading the Riding Women back to the Holdfast will be dissatisfied by *Vampire*'s departure from the first two novels' characters and settings. Worst of all, since female vampires are quite uncommon, the novel's title seems to dismiss women. The text directly announces that female vampires are not typical supernatural creatures: "Ah—what about female vampires"? The answer: "I know of none." Has Charnas set aside her interest in feminism?

Although feminism is an important part of *Vampire*, its presence is far less pervasive and extreme than in Charnas's other novels. *Walk to the End of the World* has been called "one of the best realized and most brutishly unpleasant future societies in the history of the genre." Male citizens of the Holdfast routinely exploit each other and dehumanize women. (Read "dehumanize" to encompass rape, enslavement, murder, intellectual and nutritional deprivation, and the notion that women's flesh should be used to supplement the food supply.) There is no such unpleasantness in *Motherlines*.

Vampire lacks the exaggerated utopian and dystopian characteristics of *Walk* and *Motherlines*. The novel is an appropriate next step for Charnas. No woman can be as free as the Riding Women of the Motherline tribes; no man would advocate the Holdfast's destruction of women merely because they are women. The fantastic premises of these novels have adequately articulated Charnas's feminist point of view. There is no reason for her to express herself again in this same vein. Thus, instead of creating a novel where the Riding Women gallop into the Holdfast—a novel that would not say anything that was not said by its predecessors—Charnas now writes about true-to-life feminists who inhabit the real world. Unlike *Walk* and *Motherlines*, the fantastic element of *Vampire* is not its setting but rather its protagonist, Edward Lewis Weyland, the vampire.

As Alldera's experiences within and outside the boundaries of the Holdfast reflect women's relationship to the patriarchy, the portrayal of Weyland makes comments about women—and men. With *Vampire*, Charnas has widened her scope in two significant ways: First, what characters think and how they behave is more important than their environment. Second, its feminist concerns are but one of the threads woven together to form *The Vampire Tapestry*, whose design depicts humanity. *Vampire* moves beyond, but does not exclude, feminism. I will illustrate this statement by discussing *Vampire*'s relationship to feminism. Then, I will show how the novel enhances our understanding of the larger, nonfeminist society.

Mrs. Katje De Groot, former citizen of South Africa, former faculty wife, present college custodian, and occasional vampire hunter, is not a stereotypical middle-aged woman. It is she, an intelligent, resourceful, Alldera-like figure, and not Edward Weyland, who is at the center of "The Ancient Mind at Work," the novel's first section. And it is she who connects *Vampire* with the concerns of *Walk* and *Motherlines*. Her following comment about the mistreatment of South African blacks is, for example, reminiscent of Alldera's experiences in the Holdfast: "My grandfather and Uncle Jan whipped the native boys to work like cattle and kicked them hard enough to break bones for not showing respect." Alldera was also brutally punished when she did not show enough respect for white men. Both Katje and Alldera cope with the violence that surrounds them by behaving in an animalistic fashion. Alldera reaches safety after she acts like a fleeing beast. In South Africa, Katje was a gun-toting predatory hunter who killed animals "like scarcely more than an animal herself."

Also in the manner of Alldera, when Katje leaves South Africa, she enters a new world. After becoming an American faculty wife, Katje the hunter must change her behavior to conform to her new position. (Faculty wives do not commonly carry rifles.) But after her husband dies, it is clear that Katje's status is precarious and transitory. Her economic security and high social standing die with her husband. Yet she is able to survive, to make the transition "from lady of leisure to, well, maid work." This white South African can accept her present position, which is equal to that of her coworker, a black janitor. And, although her status has fallen, our respect for her reaches new heights. A woman who spends time "vacuuming the [Faculty] Club rugs, like a farmer worn to death at his plow" certainly should receive more esteem than a pampered faculty wife who does not do any constructive work.

Katje clearly can adapt to differing circumstances, an ability she shares with Weyland: "If Weyland could fit himself to new futures, so could she. She was adaptable and determined—like him." Her determination ultimately ends the vampire's role as Professor Weyland. Because of Katje's rifle shot, Weyland is flushed from his convenient and protected life as dream researcher at Cayslin College. He must now venture into the world, interact with diversified people, and become vulnerable to them. Katje's "devastating stroke had rent him open, body and mind, and left him vulnerable to these others." Her shot is the catalyst that initiates the creation of the novel's numerous settings.

When Katje shoots Professor Weyland, as in *Motherlines*, the roles of man and beast are juxtaposed. Katje, an animallike predatory human, shoots a beast who lives in the guise of a professional humanist. And, as in *Motherlines*, this merger works to the advantage of women. Katje obtains her objective because she is a predator. "Katje de Groot the huntress whom he [Weyland] had so disastrously hunted at Cayslin College, was to have her way. Weyland would die." Katje is the only character in the novel who achieves her objective. The novel, then, ultimately proclaims the triumph of Katje.

Katje's characteristics suggest that *Vampire* signals the creation of a new, corollary genre to feminist science fiction: the feminist gothic. Her relationship with the vampire differs markedly from the following description of stock gothic characters:

> . . . the heroine is, as a rule, the central figure. She is beautiful, charming, high-minded, and modest, and blessed in the end with married happiness, usually with social position and wealth. . . . she shows the more specific characteristics of . . . an appealing softness of nature, with deep and susceptible sympathies and affections, but with an emotional instability which exposes her feelings to both the raw elements and the designs of the villainous and the cunning. She is much given to lonely musings in the forest glades. . . . She has tears at ready call. . . . As the Gothic type matured, the villain tended to displace the heroine . . . as the focus of interest. In later examples of the type, he reaches real stature and is more often than not the mainspring of the story.

Katje was apparently created in opposition to this stereotype. Flowing tears and musing alone in forest glades are simply not her style. And, as we have seen, Katje's rifle shot is the mainspring of *Vampire*. Katje literally displaces Weyland.

Katje hunts Weyland and shoots him; psychiatrist Floria Landauer listens to him and makes love to him. Dr. Landauer is a feminist nonetheless. Another assertive professional woman named Floria has appeared on literary pages: Floria Tosca. In addition to including a character created in the tradition of Floria Tosca, the novel's fourth section, "A Musical Interlude," describes the staging of the opera *Tosca*. Because the opera plays such a key role in the novel, before speaking about Floria Landauer in terms of Floria Tosca, I will digress and summarize *Tosca* for those readers who may not be familiar with that work.

Puccini's opera *Tosca*, which is based upon the 1887 play by Victorien Sardou, premiered on January 14, 1900. When the opera begins, Angelotti, a political prisoner, takes refuge in a church after he flees from Baron Scarpia, the despotic chief of the Roman police. Mario Cavaradossi is painting in the church. He stops his work to look at a miniature portrait of the woman he loves, Floria Tosca, the diva of the Roman stage. Tosca bursts into the church and arranges a rendezvous with Mario. By the end of Act One, Scarpia, in Iago-like fashion, has convinced Tosca that Mario has been unfaithful to her. In Act Two, instead of capturing Angelotti, Scarpia finds and tortures Mario. In order to save her lover, Tosca reveals Angelotti's hiding place to Scarpia. She then learns that she must sexually satisfy Scarpia to save Mario from death by hanging. Instead of cooperating with her would-be seducer, Tosca fatally stabs him. Here is Charnas's description of events in Act Two:

> This is the hour I have been awaiting! cried Scarpia. The spare, almost conversational structure of the music grew suddenly rich with the throbbing of the darker strings and brass as he disclosed the price of [Mario] Cavaradossi's life. In tones sumptuous with passion he declared his desire: How it inflamed me to see you, agile as a leopard, clinging to your lover! He sang in a voice itself as supple as a leopard's spring. At last he claimed the brazen, eager chords of lust in his own fierce voice.

At the beginning of Act Three, Mario writes a note of farewell to Tosca while he awaits his execution. The writing is interrupted when Tosca enters his cell. After hearing about how she dealt with Scarpia, Mario salutes her audacity and courage. Mario, who tries to win his freedom by playing his part in what is supposed to be his sham execution, learns that the execution is in fact no sham. After discovering that her lover is dead and facing accusations that she murdered Scarpia, Tosca jumps to her death. The curtain falls.

Both Florias are mature, successful, and sexually aggressive women. They easily make the transition from their working lives to their love lives. Neither of them fits the stereotype of the frigid professional woman. For example, Tosca says to Mario,

> Now listen: tonight I am singing,
> But the program will be brief. Wait for me
> At the stage entrance and we shall go
> Alone together to your villa.

Dr. Landauer is just as direct: "Isn't it extremely unprofessional to proposition a client?" [asks Weyland]. "Extremely, and I never do; but this now, feels right. . . . Now I want to travel all the way with you, Weyland. Let's be unprofessional together" [answers Landauer]. Weyland is not threatened by the prospect of making love to someone who is called "an ambitious woman."

How many such mature, sexy, professional female characters have appeared in literature? The creation of both Florias should be applauded. Charnas expresses her appreciation of Puccini's character by creating Dr. Floria Landauer in Floria Tosca's image. Yet, regardless of their strength of character, neither Floria is invulnerable. When Tosca learns that Mario is being tortured, we are told that "Tosca on stage was never more tragic!" And Floria the ambitious psychiatrist could benefit from professional psychiatric help: "If her friends were moving to this sort of probing and kindly advice-giving, she must be inviting help more openly and more urgently than she'd realized." Despite the two Florias' successes in love and work, they are not in control of *all* situations; like the Riding Women in *Motherlines*, they are not superwomen.

Charnas's portrayal of the vampire includes feminist insights as well as statements about the larger society. These insights and statements become clear after readers realize that we have no right to feel morally superior to Weyland. He is the hunted as well as the hunter, the victim as well as the victimizer. Like Weyland, all of us are part human, part beast. We are just as bestial as this "monstrous" vampire.

Weyland, like Floria, can be better understood when he is discussed in terms of *Tosca*, and in *Vampire*, Charnas has Weyland go to see *Tosca*. As he watches the opera, Weyland is upset by Scarpia's actions. He leaves the theater and commits murder, striking "without need, without hunger." Although this act appears to be heinous, it is important to realize that his victim is a male as opposed to the usual literary and social victim: a female. A female member of the audience watching *Tosca* is aware of how reactions differ according to a victim's gender. After seeing Tosca murder Scarpia she says, "I think what shocks them is seeing a woman kill a man to keep him from raping her. If a man kills somebody out of politics or love, that's high drama, but if a woman offs a rapist, that's sordid." In other words, because victimization is an accepted role for women, if a female character is murdered, audiences have an accepting reaction; if a female character is the murderer, audiences are shocked. And, when a male character is murdered, his death is somehow more important, more shocking, than that of a female victim. I think that Charnas, to heighten our awareness of this difference, has Weyland murder a man—not a woman, a vampire's usual victim. Hence, a muted response to Weyland's behavior is appropriate.

Scarpia, the would-be seducer, is more monstrous than Weyland. The two do have something in common, though: they both integrate nutritional appetite with sexual passion. Weyland questions, "How to distinguish appetite from passion? Or did art raise appetite to the level of passion so that they became indistinguishable?" And Scarpia says,

> . . . I crave.
> I pursue the craved thing, sate myself and cast it by,
> And seek new bait. God made diverse beauties
> As he made diverse wines. And of these
> God-like works I mean to taste my fill.

Although Scarpia's craving, satiation, and casting aside of his craved object—as well as his juxtaposition of food and sex—resembles Weyland's behavior as he hunts for human blood, the vampire shares more similarities with Scarpia's victims. Like Angelotti and Mario, Weyland is hunted by an evil pursuer who imprisons and exploits him. Weyland's evil pursuer is occultist Alan Reese. Angelotti's words, "I'm faint with exhaustion, I can't stand up" could be appropriately spoken by Weyland after Reese cages and starves him. When we see Reese victimize Weyland, it is obvious that the human occultist has more in common with archvillain Scarpia than with the "monstrous" vampire. Mario even describes Scarpia with words that could characterize Reese: "That licentious bigot who exploits the uses of religion as refinements for his libertine lust." Just as Scarpia is unquestionably the villain in *Tosca*, Alan Reese—not the vampire—is definitely the most evil character in Charnas's novel.

Both villains face similar circumstances. Like Scarpia, Reese has followers. Ironically, the nonhuman Weyland chooses to call them "Reese's creatures." And both villains are killed by one of their intended victims. After she stabs Scarpia, Tosca exclaims:

> Is your blood choking you?
> . . .
> Is your blood choking you?
> Die, accursed! Die! Die! Die!

Reese's similar end: "Weyland's bloodied hand clamped Reese's face, palm jamming the screaming mouth shut, fingers crushing the nostrils, stifling the breath. . . . All collapsed in an air-starved spasm." When Weyland kills Reese in an act of self-defense—an act that is as justifiable as Tosca's putting an end to her tormentor—he is not behaving in a stereotypically creaturelike fashion. Weyland, the vampire, is the novel's hero and, like Scarpia, the human Reese is an accursed monster. As *Walk* and *Motherlines* do not fulfill expectations of the proper roles for female characters, *Vampire* does not fulfill the expectation of a vampire's stock role.

The differences between Scarpia and Weyland suggest the blurring of distinctions between man and beast. *Vampire* specifically states that Scarpia is more bestial than human: "Maybe it wouldn't be too far off to see his [Puccini's] Scarpia as a sort of throwback to a more bestial, elemental type. . . . You're right about him being like an animal." In contrast, *Vampire* does not portray Weyland, the true throwback to a more bestial type, as a subhuman entity. Reading about him is not "like watching an animal in church pretending to be a man." It is quite the contrary. The charismatic Weyland, professor and respected scholarly author, epitomizes the popular image of a highly sophisticated individual. By referring to Scarpia, Charnas stresses the vampire's humanity. Scarpia *is* a beast; Weyland *is* human. Weyland himself recognizes his closeness to the products of human civilization: "Where did it come from, this perilous new pattern of recognizing aspects of himself in the creations of his human livestock?" As Weyland sees himself reflected by us, we, in turn, can see ourselves reflected by him. What human can say that he or she is completely devoid of bestial characteristics? After meeting Scarpia and Reese, after remembering nonfictitious evil men, who are we to pass judgment on Weyland, call him a beast, and consider ourselves to be his moral better?

Despite this point, some readers might question: How can Weyland be hailed as the novel's hero, a good human being, when he has twice committed murder? I have already justified one of his murders as Charnas's means of drawing readers' attention to the usual easy acceptance of females as victims. Weyland's first murder can also be excused: he kills to assuage the effects of starvation. Although he usually feeds upon his "human livestock" without harming them, after escaping from Reese's control, he voraciously drinks too much blood. The murder, then, directly results from Reese's desire to exploit Weyland. In addition, Weyland also should not be condemned because our society justifies killing eatable living creatures. Humans are, after all, Weyland's cattle, and we fare better with him than the livestock who meet their end in our slaughterhouses. Again, in this instance, we should not feel superior to Weyland. We love violence—and pay to see it: "Scarpia was . . . better than Telly Savalas."

Vampire Weyland's role as Professor Weyland also does not permit us to feel superior to him. His professional position is surprisingly quite violent. Professor Weyland fulfills expectations of typically vampirish behavior as he goes about his daily routine: "You're planning some politely murderous question for her [a graduate student], aren't you? All very courtly but right for the jugular." This "attack," which occurs under the guise of courteous and appropriate academic behavior, would do Dracula proud. It is not by chance that *Vampire* contains numerous direct criticisms of academe. Scholars supposedly exemplify humans at their best, humans in pursuit of truth and knowledge. In contrast, Charnas takes pains to state that the university is quite a suitable place for a vampire. And she stresses that within a system where established professors exploit the unestablished, women are especially vulnerable: "Female graduate students are so vulnerable to us [older male professors].

Weyland, the vampire who must hunt to survive, successfully applies his talents to "scholarship [which] was the best game humankind had yet invented: intricate, demanding, rich with risk and reward—akin in many ways to the hunt itself." A "game" is an apt description of what should be a serious and cooperative effort to enhance existing knowledge. Charnas further erodes the image of exalted human pursuits when she points out that the academic hunt is often neither glamorous nor spiritually elevating: Weyland's junior colleagues "hustled along trundling their little lives before them, panting and sweating to get ahead of the others just like themselves with a pull from those who trundled still further ahead. . . ." This is a degrading—and appropriate—way to describe a supposedly dignified profession.

Charnas mentions those young people who "hunger" to be a part of that profession. The following description implies that they have little hope of satisfying their hunger: ". . . young Ph.D.'s pouring out of the graduate schools panting for the jobs of older men like Weyland. . . . Peasants, these days." Vampires traditionally fear mobs of screaming peasants. Both Professor Weyland and vampire Weyland must be wary of the very same anxious hordes. Vampirelike, hallowed academic institutions do in fact drink the life's blood of their graduate students. They exploit and then cruelly cast aside such students without caring that society has no use for their academic training. Weyland as professor reminds us that we cannot justifiably place ourselves and our institutions high on undeserved pedestals.

His presence reflects the fact "that humans are also animals." Ironically, our medical institutions might cause the vampire to become the only flesh-and-blood person in the world: "Complete replacement of the body's systems by means of new technology in order to avoid death seems to be a current human goal. . . . Imagine waking from a long sleep to find people totally mechanized, myself the only 'human' (i.e., mortal) left." Thus, as I have been arguing, Charnas eradicates the definite distinctions between "creature" and "human," "hero" and "villain," "hunter" and "hunted." Despite his biological peculiarities, it is very difficult to call Weyland inhuman. He loves his cars; he seeks professional success. Are these not the characteristics of the typical contemporary American male? Most everyone who holds a B.A. must have encountered at least one equivalent of Professor Weyland. And, I daresay that women who dream about meeting a debonair, intelligent lover would certainly respond to him. He stirs something at the core of our personalities. But, despite the affection he inspires, I believe readers are relieved to see him "die."

Why? I will explain this opinion by referring to Isaac Asimov's *I, Robot*, which, like *Vampire*, is characterized by indistinct roles. In *Vampire* it is sometimes difficult to discern who is an appropriate human and who is an appropriate beast. In *I, Robot* it is sometimes difficult to discern who is an appropriate human and who is an appropriate robot. While the robots exhibit human traits, robot specialist Susan Calvin is quite robotlike. Like Weyland, these robots who resemble humans are also more long lasting than humans. They also shed light on our society: ". . . the robot as commodity brings together a good many of the social nightmares and fears of the '50s: fear of being displaced by machines; fear of being turned into machines. As a machine, the robot vampirizes the worker's brain; as a commodity, the consumer's. . . . The Three Laws stand between the reader and all that." The person as commodity also brings together a good many contemporary social nightmares and fears. Society vampirizes the individual by defining his usefulness in terms of youthful productivity and sexuality. To be old is to be invisible. In a time of paper plates and disposable diapers, people are also routinely tossed away. In Katje De Groot's words, it is as if there is someone "kicking our bodies out of the way when they're through." In still other words, what mature woman does not cringe when she sees the commercial that promises to solve the problems of skin over twenty-five? Weyland's "death" stands between the reader and all that.

The vampire's role as Weyland must end because he has become attached to people in his mind—and in his heart. "He could not hunt successfully among prey for whom he might come to care." Thus, in the end, we know that he is no longer able to use us, to vampirize us. Like Asimov's *Three Laws of Robotics*, Weyland's death also functions as a control that comforts the reader. The vampire ceases to exploit people and cast them aside when they are no longer nutritionally useful to him. On the contrary, his concern for us is so deep, he must sleep to eradicate the emotional burden of his feelings: "Now he knew with bitter clarity why in each long sleep he forgot the life preceding that sleep. He forgot because he could not survive the details of an enormous past heavy with those he cared for." His attitude is quite comforting. Even though we witness the "death" of a character with whom we can closely identify—a character whose charisma attracts us to him—his "demise" is not accompanied by our remorse. At the conclusion of *Vampire*, we are reassured to learn that the "monster" has not exploited humans after all. People have hurt him more than he has hurt them. We are no less monstrous than this scholar who is a vampire in fact.

Charnas has given new meaning to "vampire." We know that we are akin to Weyland because we both are bestial creatures who daily don a guise provided by the veneer of civilization. We have established a new rapport with him. And, in turn, he has redefined his old analogy between "human" and "food." These new definitions have been generated by emotions. Weyland the hunter, the creature who defined people as a nutritional source, once directed no emotional energy toward humanity. Humanity had a denotative meaning for him: food. "He had begun to take his prey for granted." Once Weyland begins to love and respect his prey, instead of seeing people as food, he is aware of our individuality. The tendency to concentrate upon the denotative meaning of "food" once had a survival value for Weyland. He can no longer function as a vampire when "human as food" loses its denotation. His regard for us prevents him from equating us with nutrition: "Not cattle, these; they deserved more from him than that disdain. And they had more." One who sought food under the guise of love can no longer feed when that guise is abandoned. Although love and food are metaphorically related, they cannot be combined in reality. Weyland can no longer exist because newfound meanings that are generated by newfound feelings do not have a survival value for his species. Weyland does not survive because "concern" takes precedence over "food." He sacrifices himself because he is no longer able to exploit us.

Or, rather, the vampire merely sacrifices his identity as Professor Weyland. For Weyland the sleep researcher, all of the novel's events are an unremembered dream. He will sleep, awake, and assume a new identity unable to recall his Weyland role. Floria wastes her time compiling pages of notes attempting to use psychoanalytic procedures to cure her patient. Weyland has no lengthy recallable past, no childhood. He sheds human identities like so many disposable paper products.

All of his identities have something in common though. When the vampire awakens, regardless of how he will make a living, he must undertake a specific activity; he must be an author. Like Prospero, the vampire is the architect of his own text, the creator of his own story. "He was in his own way an artist, a practitioner of the art of self-invention." No matter when he awakens, no matter what identity he assumes, his art of self-invention will be a statement that reflects specific truths about the human condition.

Although Charnas has not abandoned her feminist concerns, *Vampire* departs from her former sole focus upon them. The novel couples feminism—the earlier works' discussion of man's inhumanity to woman—with an analysis of society's bestial characteristics. Instead of portraying Alldera's return to the Holdfast, *Vampire* explains how two self-sufficient women behave in the real world. *Vampire* is neither a feminist utopia nor a feminist dystopia. It explores the true-to-life patriarchal society—and this, after all, is where the contemporary feminist must reside.

Susan M. Shwartz

MARION ZIMMER BRADLEY'S ETHIC OF FREEDOM

"You cannot take hawks without climbing cliffs."

The ironic realism of this proverb underlies Marion Zimmer Bradley's Darkover novels. For every gain, there is a risk; choice involves a testing of will and courage. Darkover—a stark world of inbred telepaths, forest fires, blizzards, and a precariously balanced ecostructure—is not one of the bliss-filled utopias that fill books of speculative fiction. Unlike such places, in which, it seems, consensus and good intentions promote social well-being, on Darkover any attempt at change or progress carries with it the need for pain-filled choice. From the very settlement of Darkover, after an accident that caused colonists to crash onto an unknown world, people accepted the necessity of deliberate choice. After all, as in Joanna Russ's *We Who Are About To*, the colonists might have chosen suicide for themselves or enforced it upon later generations by creating the highly technical, highly wasteful society that Darkover's ecology could not withstand.

But the settlers' choices, first, to live, and second, to create an agrarian, survival-oriented culture based on craftsmanship, hard work, and—much later—the psychokinetic gifts called *laran* created consequences. All later Darkovan history is the working out of those earlier choices. Have psionic talents been bred into the human line? What becomes of such people? In *Stormqueen*, Darkovans are described as deliberately breeding (or inbreeding) for laran. The results of such a dubious eugenics program are a low birth rate, oversensitized telepaths with a low sex drive, and many lethal mutations. When added to the needs of an agrarian society for healthy workers and a feudal culture's demand for pedigreed sons and patriarchal bloodlines, the society of Bradley's *Stormqueen* indeed deserves the name she gives it: the Ages of Chaos. Nor are the consequences of the choice to breed for telepathic gifts ended there. Given such complications with birth, parentage, and familial makeup, what happens to sexuality, to the lives of men and women on Darkover?

Starting from *Darkover Landfall*, in which the colony director explains how women, since their fertility is affected by forced adaptation to a new planet, must be sheltered, Bradley traces the decline of women's status from people who must be protected from hard manual labor because they are so valuable and continues (in *Stormqueen* and *Two to Conquer*) to reveal the consequences of this choice: protectiveness becomes oppression. By the time of the Ages of Chaos, women have essentially two options: to provide laran heirs or to opt out—with all the penalties that implies in a rigidly patriarchal culture—into membership in one of the sisterhoods. Underlying Bradley's work and her main theme of choice is specific emphasis on the roles of women on Darkover and the choices open to them. Since their roles are restricted, their choices are correspondingly restricted. Any choices outside the time-honored ones are laden with risk and made only with great pain and sacrifice.

The pain of choice for Darkovan women is especially apparent in *The Shattered Chain*, Bradley's novel about the Free Amazons, or, as they are more properly called, the Order of Renunciates. Though she first portrayed Amazons in *The Planet Savers* (1962) as a group of unconventional females who could work at "men's jobs" without arousing counterproductive lusts, in *The Shattered Chain*, the Amazons (or Renunciates) became a metaphor for female and human conditions on Darkover and elsewhere of being bound by old choices, refusing to remain so, and—through enduring the pain of choice—arriving at new solutions and restored integrity.

Before we examine the plot, characters, and structure of *The Shattered Chain* and show just how the theme of choice is integral to it and to Bradley's work as a whole, let us first return to her proverb: "You cannot take hawks without climbing cliffs." Compare it with the difference between the names Amazon and Renunciate. The name Amazon implies freedom. But a Renunciate—and this is the significance of the name—*renounces* something, just as the person who wants to catch a hawk gives up the safety of flat ground to venture onto the cliffs where the hawks nest. As a novel about Renunciates, *The Shattered Chain* does not entertain the idyllic optimism of books like Elizabeth Lynn's *The Dancers of Arun*, in which the dancers, male and female, practice sexual equality, a joyous communism, and the martial arts. Nor does it emphasize the alienation of women from men as does Joanna Russ in *When It Changed* and Alice Sheldon (whose pen name is James Tiptree, Jr.) in "The Women Men Don't See." Bradley's women fit—however painfully—into the context of their planet's culture. They cannot deny reality by hiding within their Guildhouses and by pretending that Darkover's code of individual responsibility has not deteriorated into a code duello in which they, as women, are automatically considered disenfranchised. Even their own charter forbids them to bear swords. And this code duello is in force in the Domains, which are the most enlightened part of Darkover. Beyond them lie only the brothels and seraglios of the Dry-Towns, where the lords' *kihar* (honor) makes the machismo of the Comyn Domains seem positively meek. As Kindra n'ha Mhari (note: Kindra "daughter of Mhari" represents the Amazons' use of matronymics), leader of a band of Renunciate mercenaries, thinks as she compares Domains and Dry-Towns:

> Ha! The Domains live under men's laws. They accept the enslavement of the Dry-Town women because it pleases them to think how benevolent, by contrast, they are to their own women. They say all men must choose their own life-styles.

All men indeed. Presumably, the women do what they are told. In relation to the way Comyn and Dry-Towners treat women, Kindra finds them little different and equally reprehensible. As Bradley tells readers, Kindra had "early freed herself from a life that now seemed to her as enslaved, as weighted with invisible chains, as that of any Dry-Town woman who walked in her ornamented bracelets and fetters of possession." Because of her own self-liberation, Kindra feels that any woman "*who truly chose*" and "*will pay the price*" could do as much.

As one of her followers, Camilla—who has chosen to be neutered and thus free herself—says, "There is always an alternative." But in the Darkover books, alternatives are predicated upon two things: sincere choice and a willingness to pay the price choice demands. *The Shattered Chain*, in terms of its structure, plot, characterization, and context within the series, is about the choices of all women on Darkover and, through them, of all people, male and female, Darkovan and Terran.

The Shattered Chain opens with a series of conflicts that directly concern women. Years after the capture of a Comyn noblewoman and the death by torture of kinsmen who tried to rescue her, she reaches out telepathically to touch Rohana Ardais, Lady of that Domain and a skilled telepath who left her work in a tower when her clan married her off. Defying her lord's ban on interference in Dry-Town affairs, Lady Rohana recruits Kindra n'ha Mhari's band of Amazons to rescue her kinswoman Melora. Because Rohana is the only one capable of telepathic communication with her, she must accompany the Amazons. So she cuts her hair, dons Amazon clothing, and attempts to adapt to Amazon ways. These actions are radical enough for a Lady of the Comyn. But she discovers that life among the Amazons is not merely a matter of wearing trousers and persevering in the face of fear. It is, as she learns, life in the face of one dramatic renunciation. And it requires a total reevaluation of all of Rohana's attitudes.

She has always been brought up to think of Domains women as privileged and Dry-Town women as oppressed. So the sight of such women makes her sick at what she regards (and what is) their actual enslavement:

> By Dry-Town custom, each woman's hands were fettered with a metal bracelet on each wrist; the bracelets were connected with a long chain, passed through a metal loop on her belt, so that if the woman moved either hand, the other was drawn up tight against the loop at her waist. . . . Some of the Dry-Town women came close and stared at the strange women with curiosity and contempt: their cropped hair, their rough mannish garb, their unbound hands, breeches, and low sandals. The Amazons, conscious of their stares, returned the gaze with equal curiosity, not unmingled with pity.

In just such a way might a twentieth-century total woman confront a woman whom, she might say, "had to work" and be regarded in return: neither understands the other's attitudes. Both are revolted. But when Rohana confides this revulsion to Kindra, she is told that,

> If they wish to suffer chains rather than lose the attentions of their men, or be different from their mothers and sisters, I shall not waste my pity on them. . . . They endure their captivity as you of the Domains, Lady,

endure yours; and truth to tell, I see no very great difference between you. They are, perhaps, more honest, for they admit to their chains and make no pretense of freedom; while yours are invisible—but they are as great a weight upon you.

Her statement is about as welcome to Rohana as 1960s radical feminists' comparing marriage to prostitution was to happily married women.

The chains that must be shattered in this story take many forms. There are indeed those chains that the Dry-Town women wear, signs of ownership, luxurious uselessness (a chained woman is one fewer person for the work force), and subjugation. But there are more subtle psychic chains as well. For example, the reason why Melora dared contact Lady Rohana was that she saw her adolescent daughter Jaelle "playing grown-up" by binding her own wrists with ribbons. Most important of all, the chains in the book are the enslaving attitudes of men and women. As a Dry-Town Lord's concubine says of the Amazons, "They're only women." Melora may be that Lord's captive, but that concubine's attitudes proclaim her his slave.

The shattering of intellectual and spiritual chains is most pronounced in Lady Rohana. Although she has hired Amazons out of desperation, she shares many of the Domains' preconceptions about them. For example, she is shocked to discover that among Amazons, the most honorable trade they can follow is that of midwife. She is surprised to learn that they do not seduce young girls, that they do not neuter women on a regular basis, and that they are kind, even motherly. Once freed of these attitudes, Rohana extends her mental liberation from the Amazons and examines her own world and the recent landing of a party of Terrans upon it. Previously, Rohana had been content to waive judgment:

> "I don't know what their trade may be, no one has bothered to tell me, though I think Gabriel [her husband] knows." She fancied a look of contempt from Kindra. *Why should I be content with ignorance? Oh, damn these Amazons, they are making me question everything*: myself, Gabriel, my very life!

Kindra's glance and wry irony in saying that a race that travels from star to star must know something worth learning point out to Rohana that, once again, she has relied on old assumptions and obeyed the laws of her husband and the royal Hasturs without thinking. When Kindra tells her that the Hasturs do not have, in her phrase, "the keeping of her conscience," Rohana wonders—not for the first time—who keeps hers. Throughout this entire first of three segments in *The Shattered Chain*, Rohana achieves two things: the rescue of Melora, who nevertheless dies in childbirth, and the command of her own conscience. She is the one who is freed.

Rohana's freedom takes the form of intellectual independence. In this new liberation, she questions most of the customs that have previously bound her. That matter, for example, of restricting telepathic work to shielded Towers and of demanding that women in those Towers be virginal: Rohana had not really wished to sacrifice her work with the matrix screens for marriage and family, yet the idea of denying her clan was unthinkable. And there had been two other women in the Tower with her. One of them was Melora, who had been kidnapped into what all perceived as slavery. But the other, Leonie, of the highest nobility in the land, "had paid the Keeper's price; she had been forced to renounce love and marriage, living in seclusion as a virgin all her life." Rohana, with regrets, had abandoned her own life in the Tower. But had any of them really had a choice? Even as Rohana realizes that the women closest to her have been compelled to live their lives by someone else's choices, she discovers the peril of her own newfound independence of thought.

This peril is intensified as Melora dies in childbirth. Because Rohana is protective of Melora's daughter Jaelle, she wishes to send the child away. But Kindra insists that she be present. "It is her right," she tells Rohana, "or are you still lying to yourself?" In accepting what must be, Rohana learns to abandon false protectiveness and to face facts: Melora chose escape in the full knowledge that she was trading her life for Jaelle's freedom. Having realized that, Rohana now refuses to participate in the ritualized vendetta between Domains and Dry-Town by killing Melora's newborn son and thus, personally, avenging Melora upon her rapist, Jalak of Shainsa.

The hideous irony of killing Melora's child, merely because it shares in its father's as well as its mother's blood and thus avenging a dead woman, revolts Rohana as Kindra states it:

> He is a male of Jalak's blood; do not your kinsmen and your foster-brother's blood cry out for revenge, that you should cherish him? Is there not blood-feud and a life between you and Jalak's son, my lady?

Indeed there is, but the idea of killing a child to avenge the sins of the father simultaneously sickens and frees Rohana. "Blood-feud and revenge are for men, Kindra," she decides. "I am glad to be a woman, and bound by no such cruel law. Let this child's life, not his death, pay for my foster-brother's death." Her statement is more than simple defiance of "men's laws." She has decided to place her own ethical judgments above the laws of clan and caste that have hitherto bound her.

Now she perceives even the smallest shibboleths of her caste as absurd and even callous. She is appalled, first, by a hired wet nurse's "invincible stupidity," which enables her to despise the Amazons—yet it is her caste's society that has enabled the wet nurse to grow up with little more mind than a milk cow. She becomes hostile in thought to her husband, whom she suspects will begin to pressure her for another child, so that Melora's son will not grow up alone. Finally, she asks the question that Kindra asked—and answered—many years ago: "Am I only an instrument to give him sons?"

At this point, Rohana faces the consequence of her intellectual freedom. If she decides that, yes, she *is* only an instrument to give Gabriel Ardais sons, she may either continue to live with him—no better than chattel herself—or she may free herself and accept the consequences of social outlawry. And if she is *not* merely an instrument to bear sons, she must decide what she is to her husband and whether her value to him is worth the having.

She has learned that even intellectual freedom—before taking any action—carries its consequences of pain and doubt. The Amazons have revealed that to her. As Rohana prepares to re-enter her own world, she realizes why it is so different from that of the Amazons: they have given up the protectors, the keepers of conscience, that Rohana has always taken for granted but which she no longer accepts. So now she has a new problem:

> Now that I know how to make my own decisions [she asks herself], will I ever be content again to let Gabriel decide for me?
> Or if I do go back, is it only because it is so much easier to do exactly what is expected of a woman of my caste?

Here Bradley demonstrates her understanding of human nature by allowing Rohana's reflections to run contrary to the preachments of those popular and critical writers who paint liberation only in the rosiest terms. For every woman who "ups and leaves" her responsibilities, there remain burdens that other people must shoulder. Kindra, for example, abandoned her children, but not the grief of leaving them. That was the price she paid for freedom. Yet to resume the old chains—Rohana almost rebels. Her maid's concern for her appearance—"there are those who would think Melora's rescue too dearly bought at the cost of my hair and my complexion"—may disgust her as a reflection of an oppressive life-style, but she would be deluding herself if she did not admit that that same life-style contained much that she appreciated, from the creams and soft garments that soothe her skin to her value to the Domains as a member of their Council.

Even when faced with Jaelle's decision to accompany Kindra into life as an Amazon, Rohana makes the choice that will shape the rest of her life: she is staying a Lady of the Comyn. Though her decision to return to "her old life and the world of women" seems a decision to return to subservience, it is actually an affirmation, not a retreat. Having experienced another life, Rohana chooses her old one because she is bound to it by responsibilities she cannot, in honor, evade. Certainly she weeps as Kindra and Jaelle leave her; freedom and moral satisfaction hurt. And serenity lies far in the future.

The second section of *The Shattered Chain* takes place twelve years later. It is centered around one of the Terrans whose presence on Darkover compels Rohana to reject willing ignorance. The Terran agent for women's customs, Magdalen Lorne, finds in her work the problem many contemporary women share—a kind of sociological schizophrenia. On the one hand, she has undergone demanding training; her work requires dedication, concentration, and—presumably—reinforcement. On the other, her success is limited on Darkover, not because of her lack of competence but because she is supervised by men who refuse to risk offending high-level Darkovan men by placing women in roles they do not consider appropriate for them.

This problem with her work is exacerbated by her abortive marriage with agent Peter Haldane. Because both Peter and Magdalen have grown up on Darkover, their social conditioning is Darkovan, though their political allegiance is Terran. This reinforces the schizophrenia because their roles—as Darkover-influenced Terrans—create destructive competition between them. Like many men and women of the twentieth century, Magdalen and Peter are caught up in a lethal double bind. As workers they become not colleagues but rivals in a system that automatically puts Magdalen at a disadvantage. She may admire Peter's ability, but she also resents the accident of gender that enables him to achieve more than is permitted her. He realizes this and, despite what might be good intentions, uses it against her. The double bind is intensified by their isolation from other Terrans. Because of their early childhood training, Magdalen and Peter react sexually as Darkovans: they have no potential mates in the worlds of the Terran Empire. Thus, while the Empire's needs drive them apart, their own early conditioning forces them back toward a reconciliation that would be disastrous.

This unpromising situation is interrupted by Rohana Ardais, who brings word to the incompetent Terran Coordinator that her son Kyril, who looks like a twin of Peter Haldane, has been lost at the same time that Haldane disappeared. Magdalen is shocked by her immediate, shared respect for the Comyn noblewoman. So is Rohana, whose telepathic power suggests to her that she and Magdalen may one day have to work together. When word comes that Peter has been mistaken for Rohana's son by a Terran-hating bandit, Rohana and Magdalen learn that both Terran and Darkovan authorities are prepared to let Haldane be killed rather than disturb the status quo. Once again, Rohana rebels.

This time she sends Magdalen out disguised as an Amazon. Neither anticipates trouble: after all, Magdalen has successfully passed as a Darkovan many times. Unfortunately, she has always passed for a highly conventional Darkovan woman, not an Amazon. In that conventional persona, Magdalen's reaction to the hardships of Amazon life all but destroy her. Nevertheless, as true Amazons do, she attempts to carry on with her mission despite her fear.

Magdalen's resourcefulness and courage are almost enough. But Rohana's ignorance of subtle Amazon customs betray Magdalen to a band of Amazons whom she meets. Rohana's carelessness puts all of them in jeopardy. Having chosen to impersonate an Amazon, Magdalen now faces the consequences of her choice: she must become an Amazon in truth by swearing the oath of the Sisterhood.

Once again Magdalen's Terran and Darkovan personas clash. To Margali, her Darkovan side, any oath is binding, even one as audacious as the oath of the Amazons. To the Terran, the oath, administered under duress, is not binding; this shocks her other half. And the consequences of that oath are staggering for either persona: the Darkovan faces being sent to a Guildhouse for training she can only consider unfeminine; the Terran sees time in a Guildhouse as failure. If she obeys the Amazons, she condemns Peter to death. Yet if she does not take the oath, she must go to a Guildhouse for judgment. As the leader of the Amazon band, Jaelle, daughter to Melora and foster daughter to Kindra, tells her, she has no choice at all.

So Magdalen, Terran by birth, Darkovan by conditioning, swears the oath under compulsion in a scene that is the actual center of *The Shattered Chain*. This oath describes just how the Amazons are indeed Renunciates and yet, paradoxically, how they attain liberation.

The oath is primarily negative in form. It begins with a series of prohibitions. The woman swearing it must renounce both ceremonial marriage and concubinage. She must give up her father's name and the protection and financial support of all men. She must swear never to bear a child for anyone's wishes except her own. Beyond allegiance to the laws of the land and to her employer of record, she renounces all clan and family ties.

However, after this series of renunciations, the Amazon swears to regard all women in her Guild as mothers, sisters, and daughters. Having renounced one family, she gains another.

Failure to comply with the oath carries harsh punishments. "If I fail," an Amazon must swear, "then may every woman's hand turn against me, let them slay me like an animal and consign my body unburied to corruption and my soul to the mercy of the Goddess."

As Magdalen takes this oath, she reflects. At first, her Terran persona is untroubled by it; no Terran would wish, or be permitted, ceremonial Darkovan marriage. But the question of renouncing men's names hurts her. "*I didn't mind giving up Peter's, when we separated,*" she thinks. "*But you, Dad, do I have to renounce you, too?*" The oath's prohibition against women's earning a living by selling sexual favors strikes her, now, as having wider consequences. Could a woman with no occupation beyond that of wife be so regarded? Magdalen's own mother, though she was a fine musician, would thus be condemned.

Other clauses in the oath distress Margali. She weeps over not having borne Peter Haldane a child. "*I wanted so to please him. I know I'd failed him—and now I can never . . . never make it up to him.*"

So Magdalen weeps as she takes the oath. She learns, in the first demonstration of sisterhood after she is finished, that many of the women who witnessed her oath took it with tears too. Her choice to take the oath has enabled her to enter a close-knit circle that she appreciates. Yet, if she obeys the oath, she condemns Peter Haldane to death. Her choice has created more pain for her: honor the oath and kill Haldane; break the oath and flee offworld to escape the vengeance of the Amazons, assuming that Peter, as Darkovan as she, would accept his life at the price of oath breaking.

Only an attack by bandits rescues Magdalen from her dilemma. During the attack, she saves Jaelle's life. While Jaelle expects that Magdalen will abandon her, she is grateful and touched that she does not. Magdalen's sisterly act earns her a reward: Jaelle chooses to accompany her to Sain Scarp, where Peter Haldane is held captive. This choice has further implications: Jaelle has now involved herself with people who are both Terran and Darkovan. If the choice liberates Magdalen and Peter, it now implicates Jaelle.

In the third and final section of *The Shattered Chain*, set primarily in Rohana Ardais's castle, Jaelle faces the consequences of all the choices of her life. Before she met Peter, she had regarded the Amazon way of life as complete liberation. In fact, she had laughed as she swore the oath. Traumatized by her mother Melora's experiences, she welcomed the oath as a certainty that she would never suffer such oppression herself. Her revulsion extends to marriage and, indeed, to all sexuality. Despite fairly early sexual activity on Darkover, Jaelle is still a virgin at the time she meets Haldane, to whom she is immediately attracted. Only Magdalen's help enables Jaelle to overcome her early conditioning and fear of "giving herself" as "an open door to bondage and slavery." Jaelle learns, as the midwinter snows compel Magdalen, herself, and Peter to remain in the castle, that for her, love is an overwhelming experience. Her choice to love forces her to reevaluate her entire life, in just the way that Rohana and Magdalen did before her. Her thoughts cause her regrets. Previously, she had regarded marriage only as "rape made lawful." Now she wishes for the secure permanence that marriage to Peter might bring her. She is sworn to have children only if she wishes them; but she also wishes to please him, and he wants children. The foundations on which Jaelle has built her life shake as she examines them.

In this examination, she gets no help from Peter, whose outlook is that of a conventional Darkovan male. In fact, he is concerned that her closeness with Magdalen could be construed as lesbian. And the presence of other men in the castle—notably her cousin Kyril and Rohana's husband Gabriel—complicate matters even more. Both Kyril and Gabriel are very much of the old school. Not only do they mistrust the Amazons, they reject them totally. Kyril's actions enrage her as he confronts her with his knowledge of her affair with Peter and assumes that, having slept with his look-alike, she can have no qualms about sleeping with him.

> "You damnable Amazon bitches," he cries, "thinking yourself free of all the rules for women, thinking that you can pretend yourself chaste ladies and demand that we treat you like chaste ladies, and then playing the whore when it suits you . . ."

Kyril invokes the double standard: Peter, his friend, may sleep with whomever he chooses, but Jaelle may not. His assumption that there are indeed rules for women shows how far removed he is from a conscious choice of values: for him old ways are good, and he has never thought of any other. For him sexuality is allied to hostility and domination; Jaelle represents a challenge to be mastered.

For Kyril, the Oath of the Amazons might as well not exist. For Kyril's father, it is a scandal. He chooses to ignore it. Even for Haldane, who loves Jaelle, it is a faintly absurd archaism that makes life with his lover slightly more difficult.

Rohana, observing the interactions of Comyn and Terran men and women, realizes that all of them fit into a pattern that may serve both worlds. She asks to accompany Peter, Magdalen, and Jaelle to Thendara, the Trade City, to confront Darkovan and Terran leaders. At Thendara, finally, Jaelle's examination of her whole life explodes into anguish. To Rohana's horror, Jaelle now feels that she took her oath too young. Now, whether she wants it or not, she is sworn to take her freedom. "At what price?" Rohana asks her. That is, indeed, the overwhelming question.

Jaelle has only now begun to realize the price of freedom. For her it had always been axiomatic that "a woman not free to choose is only a slave." Yet, as Rohana points out, the freedom to choose does not guarantee happiness. Rohana, having made her own choices, sees the Amazon oath as opposed to choice in its attempt to safeguard women against the risks that women on Darkover assume. And a riskless life is not possible. Experienced, mature, saddened by her own hardships, Rohana expresses Bradley's philosophy of choice to Jaelle: "Every woman must choose what risks she will bear." Rohana's compassionate tolerance enables Jaelle to work out a solution to their dilemmas that adheres to the terms of the oath. Amazons are oath bound to obey their employers; they may accept all legal employment. By decree of the Comyn Council, work for the Terrans is legal employment. It is not free of risk by any means, but it is a choice of which Rohana approves.

Rohana's mental image of "a great door swinging wide, both ways, an opened door between locked away worlds" is transmitted to Magdalen and Jaelle as the book ends. This door is a choice, taken in pain and renunciation, that enables people to go on to other choices that may produce joy. Opening such a door is a risk, but only through risk can true joy come.

As we see in *The Shattered Chain*, the payment for taking an oath is the payment for all such choices: pain, with a potential for achievement. In Bradley's other books, too, the price of choice is of great importance. In the books that deal with the Ages of Chaos, *Stormqueen* and *Two to Conquer*, we see Allart Hastur, cursed with the ability to see simultaneously all the consequences of all possible choices, choose among them and, because of his choices, reluctantly accept a crown. Bard di Asturian chooses to rape a woman and then must endure telepathic replay of his brutality. His suffering changes his life, forcing him into a kingship that—despite his training as a soldier—may bring peace to his kingdom. Both Allart and Bard achieve satisfaction, but it comes only at the price of great pain. Ironically enough, the satisfaction they earn is never what they thought they wanted.

Bradley's books dealing with Damon Ridenow (*The Spell Sword*, *Forbidden Tower*, and the rewritten version of *The Bloody Sun*) show how Damon Ridenow's refusal to accept Darkovan custom starts a revolution that takes three generations to accomplish. He questions the dogma that only women can be Keepers and that such Keepers must be virgins. He questions the policy of isolation from Terra. He questions the custom of confining telepathic work to a Tower. And in questioning, he meets and loves people whose children take their part in making new and painful choices. Just to mention one such child, Damon's daughter by Jaelle, the Keeper Cleindori, attempts to reshape custom on Darkover and is assassinated. Yet, in the next generation, Cleindori's son chooses to enable Terrans and Darkovans to work together and share their knowledge.

Perhaps the most personal of Bradley's examinations of choice is her work with Lew Alton and Regis Hastur in *Heritage of Hastur*. If the Amazons represent her statement on women making choices, the characters Lew and Regis are choice makers who are important, personally, to Bradley's development as a writer. Both appeared in her fiction from the time when Darkover was a series of unpublished manuscripts about a place called Al-Merdin, a pleasant amalgam of Henry Kuttner, A. Merritt, and J. R. R. Tolkien. In the Al-Merdin stories, Regis is a youth out to vindicate a friend, while Lew Alton developed into what Bradley, in the privately printed quarterly *Starstone* and an introduction to her story "Blood Will Tell" calls her animus, her private voice in her fiction.

In *Heritage of Hastur*, Regis and Lew are portrayed as interrelated as their bloodlines and the choices each must make. Structurally and emotionally they are foils to one another.

Regis begins as a prince, accepted, but not gifted with *laran*. Therefore, he regards himself as an outcast, a feeling intensified by his lack of parents and close friends. Lew, on the other hand, is a superb telepath and has experienced the closeness of a Tower circle and of a loving family, but he too feels himself an outcast because the Comyn Council has refused to regard him as more than a legitimatized heir. Neither Regis nor Lew feel as if they fit in. And they both reach the same conclusion: their lives would be simpler if they could opt out: Lew to a Tower or to his renegade kindred at Aldaran; Regis—audaciously enough—into the service of the Terran Empire.

Neither wants any part of the Comyn, which attempted to arrange their lives, marriages, careers, even their thoughts. But where Regis rebels overtly against Comyn control after his friend Danilo is disgraced, Lew rebels against his father because of a cruel misunderstanding. Their reasons for making choices thus become important because they control the choices available. Regis realizes that "he, who had once sworn to renounce the Comyn, now had to reform it from inside out, single-handedly, before he could enjoy his own freedom." His choice is to rebuild.

Lew's choice, however, is to break with his father and the Council and ally instead with the Aldarans, who propose to replace the Council. This rebellion implicates him in what Darkovan aficionados know as the Sharra rebellion, a struggle for power involving a fearfully powerful psychokinetic crystal. The use of this crystal, embedded appropriately in a sword, allegedly will enable Lew and his allies, his cousin Beltran of Aldaran and the enigmatic Robert Kadarin, to bring the blessings of technology to a Darkover that really does not want them. But, as a venerable *leronis*, or telepathic adept, tells Kadarin, "If you have any flaw, it will expose it brutally; if you seek only power, it will turn your purposes to such ruin as you cannot even guess; and if you handle its fires recklessly, they will turn on you and consume you and all you love!" This crystal is to be entrusted to Lew, whose motives are rebelliousness and alienation. Abetted by the power-hungry Beltran and by Kadarin, what Lew achieves is the fulfillment of the adept's prophecy. Because his motivation was negative, his choice is negative—and its consequences are disastrous.

As Regis persists in his one-man quest to reform the Comyn, he discovers that the only way to reform it is to stay with it. Even as Lew's health and sanity drive him offworld—a fate he, unlike Regis, never dreamed of—Regis must swear away his dreams of adventure in far star systems by taking a lifelong oath to serve the Comyn as heir to Hastur and the Regency. In a powerful scene before the entire Comyn Council, Regis swears his oath; not, like Lew, in anger, but in full knowledge that he is swearing away his freedom.

He knows now that he will never see the stars. Is this his choice? he is asked. It is. "Not his wish," says Bradley, "but his will, his choice. His fate." Like Allart Hastur before him, Regis takes on the burden of responsibility he does not want. And like the women in *The Shattered Chain*, he accepts the fact that on Darkover, choice consists not so much of shattering chains but of choosing what chains will bind him. Choice compels him to shoulder increasingly arduous burdens. And, like Rohana before him, Regis sees how these duties may produce satisfaction. He uses even his own pain to help a friend, as when he attempts to comfort Lew:

> And then, out of his own forfeited dreams and hope, out of the renunciation he had made, still raw in his mind, he offered the only comfort he could, laying it like a gift before his friend:
> "But you have another world, Lew. And you are free to see the stars."

Lew travels widely. At the end of *The Sword of Aldones*, he is depicted as an exile. Regis becomes, essentially, the savior of Darkover by participating (*The World-Wreckers*) in an alliance with Terran telepaths and science. Neither is completely satisfied. Each has lost too much for that. But as Rohana Ardais, wisest of all of Marion Zimmer Bradley's characters, says, "I did not say I had no regrets . . . only that everything in this world has its price, even such serenity as I have found after so many years of suffering." Like Regis, Rohana has everything she wants but her freedom. That would have cost too much. Nevertheless, what they both make of what they have is Darkover's salvation and a tribute to Bradley's realistic understanding and exposition of human psychology.

Edgar L. Chapman

SEX, SATIRE, AND FEMINISM IN THE SCIENCE FICTION OF SUZETTE HADEN ELGIN

The science fiction novels of Suzette Haden Elgin adopt a formulaic plot structure to examine some profound and intriguing themes. Elgin's fiction often treats issues that may be considered feminist in nature, but to stereotype her work as feminist would be an injustice. In addition to describing the social and political status of women, Elgin's fiction raises serious questions about religion and the uses of power. In fact, Elgin's work often indicts future societies that—not unlike our own—are willing to exploit human beings for the perpetuation of a social and bureaucratic order.

The central figure in Elgin's first four science fiction novels is the "inter-galactic secret agent," Coyote Jones. Jones, a maverick and something of a picaresque hero who works for the Tri Galactic Intelligence Service several centuries hence, roams over Elgin's universe and provides not only a unifying link in the stories, but also a common humanist consciousness for them. Before examining the themes of Elgin's fiction, therefore, it will be useful to take a look at Jones and to define his role in her novels. Then we shall turn to individual works and finally to comments on the relationship between the Coyote Jones novels and the Ozark Fantasy Trilogy.

Coyote Jones, Elgin's hero, is something of an antihero, conceived in the sixties mold of James Bond and other prominent heroes of popular culture. Jones has a liberal mentality, a very active libido, and an innate irreverence for authority. His encounters with his boss, The Fish, who is the government official in charge of the Tri-Galactic Intelligence

Service, provide much of the humor in the books. Unlike Bond, however, Jones's sense of humor is never smug or cruel and, again unlike Bond, Jones is neither a sexual chauvinist nor a man of violence. Instead of a license to kill, Jones possesses extraordinary psi powers: as a "mass projective telepath," he can influence crowds or even whole populations by broadcasting telepathic concepts and imagery. If need arises, Jones can get out of a tight spot by inciting a riot or a strike, although as a compassionate humanist, he does not want to harm the victims of his illusions; and as a conscientious professional agent, it is not in his interest to create disorders that might attract attention.

Elgin, together with giving Jones power as a projective telepath, gives him a weakness, although it is a defect that has a compensating value. Jones can send out telepathic images and concepts, but he cannot receive them: He is "mind-deaf," a condition that arouses pity and contempt in some fellow telepaths, like Dean O'Halloran of *Star-Anchored, Star-Angered*. On the other hand, Jones's imperviousness to other telepathic signals is not complete, for he does respond to the projections of the beautiful "mind-wife" or geisha woman on Furthest. Moreover, this mind-deafness has the virtue of rendering Jones almost invulnerable to the attacks or illusions of other projective telepaths. This is not entirely true, however, for Tzana Kai, the female telepath who is Jones's closest friend and lover, is capable of stunning his brain with telepathic "sendings" in their occasional lovers' quarrels.

Jones's relationships with women create considerable interest in the novels. Set in a distant time when most citizens of the three galaxies enjoy an enviable degree of sexual freedom, the series assumes that numerous sexual liaisons are the rule. Standards of dress are very liberal, for most people wear loincloths or similar light clothing. On the whole, the novels reflect the sexual attitudes of the sixties and early seventies, presented generally without criticism. In this context, Jones could be expected to have numerous affairs, and he does enjoy sexual interludes on his assignments. He has a torrid romance with Bess, the mind-wife on Furthest, becoming the father of her child, whom he then decides to rear after her death. In *At the Seventh Level*, Jones deflowers the virginal poet, Jacinth, at her request; and in *Star-Anchored, Star-Angered*, Jones establishes a platonic love relationship with the female prophet and messiah, Drussa Silver. Yet throughout the series, Jones's most enduring relationship with a woman is that with Tzana Kai, his fellow agent, a charming and strong-willed woman to whom he always returns. Coyote Jones relies on her advice, her intelligence, and her independent judgment on several occasions, and at least once, in *At the Seventh Level*, he thinks of her professional advice with a rueful approval. Having foolishly become a captive of a criminal, Jones thinks of Tzana's statement that: "Curiosity . . . is only useful as an intellectual vice. When it becomes a matter of the passions, as it is with you, it ceases to be simply a tool of the mind, and becomes a way of getting oneself killed." For her part, Tzana displays as much sexual liberalism as Jones; in fact, if anything, she is depicted as having enjoyed many more lovers. Yet, like Jones, her persistent emotional attachment is found in their relationship. Elgin seems to view the ideal sexual relationship as much like this one: a comic battle of wits and personalities involving strongly erotic feelings.

If Jones is a sexually liberated man, he is equally independent and liberated—contemptuous might be a better word—in his attitude toward authority. Espionage is not his first choice of profession; rather, the Tri-Galactic Intelligence Service has chosen him on the basis of his highly unusual telepathic talents. In the future world in this series invented by Elgin, the universe is supposed to be governed democratically, and the forms of democracy are elaborately observed (everyone calls everyone else "Citizen," as in the first years of the French Revolution); but the reality behind the formality is a government much like our contemporary American one, where bureaucracy and a rather obvious power structure actually manage things more or less to their liking.

Jones is thus a reluctant spy and hero, obliged to work for the interplanetary intelligence service simply because it is the most convenient way to avoid trouble and gain rewards for his intelligence and his psi or telepathic powers. His disenchantment toward his work makes Jones more sympathetic for the reader; for despite his romantic aura, the spy is not always a very pleasant figure, even in naive popular mythology. Moreover, as a compassionate and sometimes quixotic humanist, Jones often shows resentment about being asked to investigate people or a humanoid species for whom he feels respect or for whom he develops affection. In fact, Jones's chief failing as an agent—his proclivity to get involved emotionally with the beings he is investigating—is one of his most endearing qualities as a human.

Indeed, Jones shows his naturally rebellious nature and his tendency to develop emotional attachments throughout the series. At the end of

The Communipaths, Jones tries to join the Maklunite religious cult and abandon his profession. In *Furthest*, Jones's involvement with the rebel mind-wife, Bess, leaves him with a daughter to raise, a task he accepts with genuine enthusiasm, if with poor preparation. Also in *Furthest*, Jones not only learns what he was sent to find out, but he decides to use his report to influence the Inter-Galactic Council and ultimately to reform the planet's social structure. Finally, though unable to change the sexual chauvinism on Abba in *At the Seventh Level*, Jones does become a strong spokesman against the subjugation of women.

Jones's individualism, his independence, his dislike for bureaucracy, and his tendency to form emotional bonds on the planets he visits, are presented as a strong contrast to his superior in the Tri-Galactic Intelligence Service, The Fish. The Fish is, like many popular depictions of intelligence czars, an aloof and emotionally detached man who tends to see humans as objects or as so many chess pieces to be moved around. But though Elgin follows popular literary stereotype in her portrayal of The Fish, she does give him the saving grace of some self-deprecating humor, and she humanizes him with some small but amusing touches of male vanity. On the whole, he serves as a good foil for Jones.

Jones is clearly no superman, and, as I have indicated, he is sometimes a bit of a rogue and antihero. Yet he is a credible male hero, not a cardboard superman or a two-dimensional comic-book figure. A tall, red-bearded fellow with an earthy and folksy idiom, perhaps reflecting Elgin's Missouri childhood, Coyote Jones is a moral humanist in the guise of an adroit picaresque trickster.

It is sometimes contended by male critics that women writers have difficulty creating believable heroes or, for that matter, credible male characters. There may be scant truth in this argument, at least where many celebrated women writers are concerned. (The converse argument, that male writers do not create very believable or sympathetic women characters, has been both popular and fashionable with some feminist critics in recent years. This contention is probably equally false.) But some women writers working in such popular forms as the mystery or the thriller do much to justify it. According to the traditional argument, women writers tend to imagine male heroes who are impossible fantasy figures—for instance, either the woman's dream lover or the powerful masculine figure whom she would like to be.

However, this ancient and probably sexist criticism does not apply to Elgin's Coyote Jones. Even if there is a bit of fantasy involved in his creation, he remains a credible male character with whom men can identify. When this is established, though, we may go on to say that the novels contain a good deal of intellectual interest.

In *The Communipaths* (1970), the first novel in the series, Elgin establishes a conflict between the Maklunite religious cult and the state, in this case the Tri-Galactic Federation. The chief feminine protagonist, Anne-Charlotte, a member of the Maklunite cult, violates the rules of her religion and government precept by having a baby without permission. The baby, who is possessed of extraordinary psi powers, is taken away from her by the state, and the novel moves fitfully toward tragedy. Eventually Anne Charlotte goes mad, despite the loving care of her coreligionists, and finally commits suicide. Her baby, because of her telepathic powers, is supposed to be trained to be a "communipath," or state telepath used in facilitating inter-galactic travel—an unenviable fate because communipaths have a life expectancy of eighteen because of the arduous strain on their psychic energies. However, Anne-Charlotte's baby, a mutant who insists on calling herself Susannah, turns out to be a superior telepath who will experience longevity, and, perhaps, it is hinted, even manage to change the short life span of communipaths.

Thus Elgin introduces two themes that are persistent elements of her fiction: the clash between private religious vision and the state and the martyrdom of intelligent and independent women—themes treated more effectively in her following novels. The first of these themes appears in Elgin's intriguing creation of the Maklunite cult, a romantic religious community founded on the principle of complete sharing of property, self, and even mind (for those given telepathic powers—and nearly everyone has some meager abilities of this kind in Elgin's fiction). The Maklunites are treated sympathetically, although there is some gentle humor at their expense in the diary of Tessa, an adolescent member of the Maklunites.

The Maklunite cult stresses emotion and gentle love as opposed to intellectual activity or a complex mythology. Each member of this utopian sect is admitted by group election, and he or she is expected to be master of some handicraft or skill that will contribute economically. There is, of course, a strong parallel between the hippie communes that flourished in the sixties and the Maklunites as well as reminders of the numerous utopian communities that have appeared in the American past, from the Oneida community in New York to New Harmony, Indiana. Elgin's vision in the novel suggests that such religious communities are attractive and socially benevolent but are also too naive and romantic to transform the world or exert much social influence. It is significant that an individualist like Coyote Jones is not able to qualify for a Maklunite "cluster," even though he expresses his intention to join at the end of *The Communipaths*.

Elgin's other theme, the martyrdom of imaginative or superior women, occurs in the tragedy of Anne-Charlotte. Her flaw, or crime, in the eyes of the government, is her need to express her love in parenthood to her own child. Her inability to be reconciled to a world where her baby is taken from her because of a violation of law leads to her madness and suicide. These tragic events imply Elgin's criticism both of a powerful bureaucratic government and of the Maklunite beliefs; for despite the beauty of Maklunite ideals and the sincerity of their actions, communal love proves to be no substitute for family and maternal expression of love.

Though *The Communipaths* contains such serious intellectual themes, it is not a very memorable novel. As a tragic victim, Anne-Charlotte arouses pity, but she is too passive to stir much emotion. Even the role that Coyote Jones plays seems secondary: Jones is forced to assist in taking Anne-Charlotte's child from her, an action he despises, and he is unable to change or influence very greatly the later events in the book. On the whole, Elgin's first published novel shows some uncertainty of intention and focus, although it contains much effective writing and establishes a formula of considerable potential.

The next novel in the series, *Furthest* (1971), is much stronger. Here Jones goes to another distant planet, this time on the very edge of the known universe—hence the name Furthest, which also gives the book its awkward title. Furthest is a planet where archaic mores appear to reign. The inhabitants are formal and even Victorian in dress and speech, and their sexual prudery is renowned. Eventually, however, Jones learns that the society on the planet's surface is a sham, a misleading illusion aimed at hiding the fact that the Furthesters are actually an aquatic people, descendants of a mating centuries ago between a humanoid species and intelligent fishlike creatures resembling dolphins. Certain members of the Furthest population are conscripted for surface duty to maintain the subterfuge. The analogies with the military draft are strong.

After learning the truth, Jones returns home to report and convinces his chief and the Tri-Galactic Council to arrange a program of quarantine for the planet, during which its inhabitants can gradually be educated into an accommodation to the more liberal life-styles of the Tri-Galactic world. As usual, Jones acts in the role of the enlightened humanist, hoping to shield a more primitive society from culture shock, while preserving its artifacts and life-style for the study of anthropologists.

While this is the major plot in *Furthest*, most of the drama arises from a secondary conflict involving Jones's relationship with Bess, a rebellious mind-wife. Mind-wives are female telepaths given special state training to become skilled mental prostitutes: they use thought waves to provide sexual ecstasy for their clients. Elgin describes Jones being given a purely mental orgasm by Bess:

> He had time for only that one thought, and then the sprays of gold began behind his eyes, curling and uncurling, forming intricate dancing patterns that swooped toward him up to the last impossible instant before they burned him alive, grew and grew into roses of tender gold blossoming into fountains, and then burst into trailing golden dust, chiming as they broke.

Elgin attempts to render this experience in a lyrical tone, yet her imagery is rather traditional in description of sexual ecstasy. It is to Elgin's credit that she is perhaps the first science fiction writer to attempt to describe the sexual possibilities of telepathy. But her imagery does not differ markedly from what she might have used to depict a more carnal form of copulation. Later we learn that Bess becomes Coyote Jones's lover in the more ordinary physical sense, and Elgin presents this event as an action that makes their relationship more fulfilling and satisfying. In short, although the possibilities of telepathic sexual experience are depicted as exciting, mental sex appears rather limited. Bess is a highly trained courtesan or geisha, and the pleasures she provides for Jones are a kind of sensual pleasure (for want of a better phrase) of a special variety. In this affair, Bess's initial mind encounter with Jones serves only as an overture to a more complete emotional involvement.

Bess is one of Elgin's most interesting characters. Trained to be a high-class prostitute, she is a cheerful rebel against her vocation as a mind-wife. Irreverent and given to sardonic humor, Bess displays a kind of mocking insolence toward her former exploiters that wins our admiration. Accused of a crime against religion, Bess's real transgression is her desire to overthrow the entire social system of her planet, or at any rate end the exploitation of female telepaths that turns them into government prostitutes.

It is inevitable that Bess's rebellion should end with her defeat. Although she finds refuge for a time with Jones as his friend and lover, she is eventually captured and punished by "Erasure"—a complete abolition of mind and memory, virtually a form of execution although it spares the body. Her psychological death occurs while Jones, her protector, is absent from the planet on business. On his return he finds that her death has a self-sacrificial character: the birth of their child betrayed Bess, but even in her confession she managed to mislead the authorities in order to protect Jones and her younger brother from implication in her "crimes."

Like the gentle Anne-Charlotte in *The Communipaths*, Bess, the revolutionary, is one of Elgin's heroic and martyred women. As I have observed, Elgin's fiction is dominated by the theme of superior women martyred by an indifferent society, usually one dominated by a masculine bureaucracy or a patriarchal religion. Frequently, the woman is a telepath or has extraordinary psi powers—a science fiction symbol of the artist or a person with extraordinary talents. The tragedy of Bess is a more memorable and heroic treatment of this theme than the tragedy of Anne-Charlotte in *The Communipaths*; hence *Furthest* is a stronger novel.

Elgin's next novel, *At the Seventh Level* (1972), written and published at the high tide of the contemporary feminist movement, is very well crafted and polished. Yet it is curiously disappointing. The novel takes Coyote Jones to the planet Abba, where male chauvinism reigns supreme in a kind of imitation (or parody) of Arabic culture. There is a good deal of enjoyable satire in the novel, and Jones becomes an effective spokesman for sexual equality. But I have the impression that an overtly sexist society like Abba is much too easy a target for Elgin with her talent for comedy and satire. After all, few responsible thinkers would consciously admire the Abban society or defend it, although, of course, men may allow themselves to enjoy fantasies of women on their knees, always ready to gratify male sexual desire. It is possible, however, that Elgin was not only making a direct feminist statement but was also replying to the juvenile sexist science fiction (or fantasy) of writers like John Norman, with his Gor series.

The plot of *At the Seventh Level* concerns Jones's visit to Abba on assignment to investigate the apparently systematic poisoning of Jacinth, a brilliant woman poet (only the third such in ten thousand years). In the prologue, "For the Love of Grace," originally published as a separate short story, we learn of Jacinth's struggles to become a poet and her father's opposition to this goal and chagrin at her success. Elgin's satire on sexual chauvinism is at its most biting in her portrait of the Khadilh, Jacinth's stupid and sexist father, an important official embarrassed by his daughter's brilliance. To the Khadilh's dismay, Jacinth not only qualifies as a poet in a rigorous test—when failure would mean a lifetime of solitary confinement—but she attains the highest rank, the seventh level.

In Abban society, women are not permitted to enter any other professions than poet, except those of wife, mistress, or prostitute, although there are several varieties of the latter. Hence a brilliant woman like Jacinth has only the choice of risking the examination for poets if she is to escape a life of intellectual and social inferiority. That fate is portrayed by two sheeplike women whom the government provides Jones for sexual companionship.

To his credit, Jones refuses to take advantage of these docile exploited creatures. Part of his reaction is not so much moral, as psychological and sexual: Jones belongs to a certain breed of intelligent men who have trouble feeling desire for a woman unless she displays marked intelligence and a challenging personality.

While fending off his docile female companions, Jones encounters some difficulty in solving the mystery of the supposed poisoning. On Abba, crime is legal, as long as professional criminals register with the government—another of Elgin's satirical thrusts at centralized bureaucracies. At one point, the analogy with our world is stressed, when Jones comments:

> There can be no law—and no justice, my friend—in a society where any law may be broken as long as the proper form has been filled out first. That system prevailed on old Earth for centuries, and came very

near bringing about the destruction of the human race on that planet. It works no better now than it ever did.

Yet, it turns out to be a fundamentalist religious cult that is harming the poet Jacinth, not by poison but by a combined mind probe. These poor souls are appropriately punished by Jones's telepathic powers; he brainwashes them into near idolatry of Jacinth. Here again, we see Elgin expressing scepticism about the value of religious cults and particularly conservative religious fervor since it is associated with distrust of women.

Elgin's strongest comments on the subjugation of women come at the end of the novel in a speech by Jones and in a satirical epilogue. Jones is conversing with his lover, Tzana Kai, with whom he enjoys some epic battle-of-the-sexes debates:

> "I'm just trying to get the nasty taste out of my mouth and head."
> "What nasty taste?"
> "The nasty taste of subservient women," he crooned. "Nasty, foolish, docile, subjugated, subservient women, with no minds of their own, and no thoughts to put in them, if they had any! The Light be praised, I'm back here once again with you, just as you are—obnoxious, arrogant, pigheaded, overbearing—"

Elgin here follows a time-honored satirical strategy, often used effectively in the plays of Bernard Shaw: the condemnation of male chauvinism comes from a sexually vigorous man, a strategy much like using a professional soldier to condemn war or a multimillionaire capitalist to criticize flaws in the capitalist system.

In the satirical epilogue, Elgin is only slightly more subtle in condemning male supremacist attitudes. Here Elgin depicts Jacinth, the poet, being called in to solve a problem of communication between the Abbans and another species who possess a high-protein crop necessary to Abba's economic success. The difficulty yields to Jacinth's superior linguistic skills and knowledge, leaving the government leaders of Abba with the embarrassing situation of trying to rationalize to themselves how a mere woman could show more brains and practical wisdom than they. But the epilogue closes on an ironic note: the Abban leaders are busy thinking of new reasons to exclude Jacinth, and all women, from the opportunity to exercise political power.

At the Seventh Level is Elgin's most overtly feminist book, yet despite some effective satire, it is less impressive and less interesting as art—or even as a formula adventure story—than *Furthest*. Sexual chauvinism as practiced on Abba is much too obvious a target for Elgin, and her imagination functions more effectively when her satire and sense of the comic are strongly balanced by a more affirmative romantic vision.

After *At the Seventh Level*, Elgin's science fiction writing slackened for most of the rest of the seventies. Academic duties and scholarship in linguistics during her years as a professor at San Diego State University occupied much of her energies. In 1979, however, Coyote Jones returned in *Star-Anchored, Star-Angered*, which is by far the best novel in the series. This time Elgin's themes of religious vision in conflict with society and the martyrdom of superior women crystallize in a fascinating story of a female prophet and messiah.

Star-Anchored sends Jones on a mission to investigate a new religious cult on Freeway in the hope that he can prove that the woman leader of the Shavvies is performing phony miracles. But the novel is rich in satiric overtones and more complex than the earlier ones. Jones first encounters an assertive female dean of a "multiversity" (one of the few remaining), and some acidulous satire on academia follows. Yet despite her overbearing nature, the dean is permitted some sympathy, for she is a secret, and rather Machiavellian, member of the Shavvies, the new cult with its visionary faith that is causing so much trouble.

On Freeway, Jones becomes involved in a conflict between Drussa Silver, the messianic leader of the Shavvies, and the conservative power structure, led, ironically, by a forceful woman, Tayn Kellyr (the real power on the planet's Council of Eight since the official head is a male nonentity). It seems that the class system on Freeway depends very strongly on a conservative religious establishment, for the incomes of the aristocracy are largely derived from obligatory tithes, a tax in the form of religious contributions. But Drussa Silver's Shavvy movement is causing defections from the establishment faith and, therefore, a reduction in contributions. Hence there is the need to discredit her or destroy her influence.

Although Jones is accustomed to being in the middle of such struggles and often takes the part of a misunderstood underdog, he approaches religious leaders like Drussa Silver with a habitual skepticism. But this time he comes to scoff and remains to pray. Drussa Silver proves to be not only a woman of extraordinary psi powers but also

a true "avatar of the divine." Jones's boss, The Fish, earlier remarked
in a conversation with the feminist dean that all the famous incarnations
of divinity have hitherto been men; but he is grudgingly prepared to
concede the possibility of a female prophet or messiah. Later, Dean
O'Halloran and a student discuss the theory of a contemporary feminist, Ann Geheygan, in her book *Woman Transcendent*, a treatise that
offers a corrective to The Fish's remarks:

> "First principle": she said, "that women achieve with ease that state
> of transcendence which men are able to attain only through great effort.
> Geheygan was, I believe, the first to name this state *surpassment*."

However, according to this theory, men have suppressed the female
talent for religious vision since prehistoric times, recognizing it as a
threat to masculine dominance.

Whatever we think about this, there is a history of male antagonism
to women as priests and prophets to lend it some support. At any rate,
Elgin uses the idea to provide an intellectual framework for Drussa
Silver's work as a messianic visionary. When Jones finally meets Silver,
he finds her to be an authentic Christ-figure performing genuine miracles. Jones, a man with some religious longings of his own—as we
noted, he made an effort in an earlier book to join the Maklunites—is
able to recognize the authentic numinosity of Drussa Silver's person
and the vision she serves. He becomes a willing convert, although his
response to her is not without some elements of romantic feeling.

Despite an effort to protect Silver, however, Jones cannot save her
from the inevitable murder plotted by the religious establishment (to
protect "Old Faith," as it is called). Silver is killed by a professional
"Singer," Analyn, ostensibly to preserve the establishment religion but
actually manipulated by Tayn Kellyr, the ruling force on the planetary
council. But it is an assassination that Drussa Silver accepts to complete
her messianic role; like the Jesus of the New Testament, she has the
power to save herself but chooses to die for her gospel.

At the novel's end, a chastened Jones returns home to reflect on his
encounter with the divine. His visit to the murderess Analyn has shown
her determined to punish herself by becoming a mind prostitute, and
it is clear that Dean O'Halloran and other followers of Silver will spread
her legend and her message of love throughout the three galaxies.

Star-Anchored, Star-Angered thus proves to be an ambitious revision of the gospels, with women playing the major roles: not only the messiah, but Caiphas and Judas have been cast as women, while in another sex reversal, Coyote Jones is a reluctant Mary Magdalene. The obvious comment about *Star-Anchored* would be that it presents a feminist revision of the New Testament in a science fiction form. This view is true insofar as the novel depicts a passion play with feminine protagonists; but it should be remembered that Drussa Silver's gospel is a universal message of love and divine power. Her gospel is not for women only. Actually, the most significant "feminist" theme in *Star-Anchored* is its identification of women as the sex with the greater access to transcendence and religious vision. The novel shows that Elgin is in fact more concerned with remaking religious myth than with doctrinaire feminist politics, although, of course, the two may be difficult to separate at some level. At any rate, *Star-Anchored* shows that Elgin is able to go far beyond the limits of fomulaic adventure in the Coyote Jones novels.

In Elgin's most recent work, she has abandoned Coyote Jones for a new and more ambitious design, the Ozark Fantasy Trilogy, of which two novels had been published by 1981, *Twelve Fair Kingdoms* and *The Grand Jubilee*. The composition of this trilogy has been accompanied by a departure from academic life and a move to the wilds of northeastern Arkansas, which would seem to be a kind of return to her roots for Elgin.

In the Ozark Fantasy Trilogy, the main theme is the initiation of a young magician or visionary, Responsible of Brightwater, and her efforts to preserve the Confederation, a political unity of several continents on the planet Ozark. Responsible is a lively heroine, and the writing in these books is vigorous. Although ostensibly set in the same universe as the Coyote Jones novels, Ozark is a pastoral world populated by southern mountain clans living on continents with names like Mizzurah, Kintucky, and Marktwain. This fantasy trilogy emphasizes magic rather than science, like most twentieth-century fantasy novels, and it allows Elgin to develop a richly comic and pastoral vision of lush natural plenitude and elaborate duels of magic. More than the Jones novels, the Ozark trilogy draws on Elgin's personal magic well of folk humor and folk ballads. They allow her to use the rich and homely

Ozark idioms she no doubt heard in her youth, and they permit her not only as a novelist, but as a linguistic scholar, to develop the possibilities of language inherent in her setting. Since only two of the novels have been published at this writing, it is impossible to make any final evaluation of the trilogy. Nor does space permit a detailed examination of the first two novels. But it is safe to say that the books bear witness to the continuing vitality and richness of Elgin's imagination, and perhaps a new flowering of her talent.

Suzette Haden Elgin has been a subtle feminist, one who has seldom forgotten her obligations as a novelist or artist. In addition, she has the saving grace of a sense of humor. She realizes that satire and comedy may be more effective strategies than angry rhetoric.

Elgin's work would be different if it were the fiction of a more overtly engaged feminist. But it would be less rewarding and probably less helpful to the cause of intellectual women. Elgin's fiction is indeed the work of a dedicated feminist, but it is a fiction rich in intellectual interests and concern for authentic values, whether in religion or sexual relationships. Elgin's novels display her gifts for comic character and event to great advantage, and they reveal a talent for satire that demonstrates scorn for the pompous and spurious, whether in government, the university, or human affairs. It is a talent notable in the work of another author born in Missouri, Mark Twain, and at her best, Elgin's comic and satirical effects exhibit the mocking spirit of Twain's work.

9

Carl Yoke

FROM ALIENATION TO PERSONAL TRIUMPH: The Science Fiction of Joan D. Vinge

> But she wore the nomad's tunic she had brought back with her from
> Persiponë's, the only clothing she owned, its gaudy color as alien as she
> suddenly felt herself, among the people who should have been her own.

These lines from the "footrace" scene in Joan Vinge's *The Snow Queen*
clearly express the psychological alienation of Dawn Moontreader Summer, the novel's heroine. Though she stands in a crowd of people from
her own clan, she feels that she is an outsider, that she is somehow
divorced from the very culture in which she was raised. This is the
fundamental experience of a person alienated, estranged, or disenfranchised. Any doubts about the nature of Moon's feelings are quickly
erased by a closer examination of the scene, which Vinge has skillfully
filled with clues to induce such a conclusion.

The first comes as Moon waits for the race to begin. She suddenly
feels a "tension" wrap around her "like tentacles," and to avoid it, she
moves to the front of the forming field of runners. Though she believes
the tension has been generated by a "certainty" that she will be chosen
Summer Queen, that very possibility is born from the differences
between her and the Summers. The tension she feels is symptomatic
of the anxiety felt by an alienated person, and withdrawal from it is
the typical reaction to it.

But there are other clues to establish Moon's alienation. While strug-
gling to maintain her balance amid "the jostling mob of colored ribbons
and eager Summer faces," for example, she describes them as

"strangers." Moreover, while they are dressed in traditional Summer holiday garments, she is not. She wears instead a heavy Winter's nomad tunic. Though she is struck by the irony of the situation, she somehow feels it is appropriate. Further, to disguise her resemblance to Arienrhod, the reigning Winter Queen and her biological mother, she covers her head with a scarf. The other runners are bareheaded. And, since she displays no family totem as the others do, some of the Summers challenge her right to run, which forces her to bare the sibyl symbol tattooed on her throat. In addition to identifying the sibyls, the tattoo, a barbed trefoil, is the ancient symbol for biological contamination.

If nothing else, the fact that she is a sibyl would alienate her from everyone else. Viewed as seers by some and as witches by others, sibyls are simultaneously revered and feared. Obscured by time and superstition, the actual function of the sibyls is as vehicles for the transmission of Old Empire culture. When the Empire collapsed because of civil war, a group of selfless scientists, hoping for a rapid return to civilization, created a massive databank of knowledge in every area of human concern and genetically altered certain humans so they could tap into it. Able to pass this ability on to their children, these individuals (sibyls when trained in the use of their gift) suffer from a peculiar side effect. They can infect other humans with their blood, producing madness in some and death in others. This effect has given rise to the legend that it is death both to kill a sibyl and to love one. In turn, this has caused the Winters to ban all sibyls from the capital city of Carbuncle.

Yet another mark of Moon's alienation occurs when she is struck by the irony of her parentage as she waits for the race to begin. She was neither her mother's child nor Arienrhod's. As the clone of Arienrhod, she was raised by another, a Summer. Thus, she has roots in both cultures. This, plus the fact that she is a child without a father, makes her unlike anyone else in the crowd. It is the sudden recognition of her uniqueness and her divorce from both cultures that prompts her to question what she is doing there.

Another clue to Moon's alienation is found in her reaction as Fate Ravenglass performs the final bit of ritual in the choosing of the Summer Queen at the end of the scene. A part of her mind separates from the rest, and while she participates in the ceremony, she also experiences near panic from her sudden doubt that she will be chosen. Momentarily, she falls into "Transfer," that state sibyls experience when they are in contact with the Old Empire computer, then she is snapped to wakefulness and finds herself in Fate's body. She watches the candidates for Summer Queen file by, but she is barely able to see them because of Fate's near blindness. Then, she sees herself stumbling forward, supported by two other women, and she reaches out and masks herself. Immediately she is snapped back into her own body, and she realizes that Fate is also a sibyl. This experience of separateness is schizophrenic and that is exactly where modern psychiatry classifies cases of extreme self-alienation. Moreover, she also realizes that indeed she is being controlled, that she is being programmed through her experiences, and that her destiny is truly not hers to control.

Moon's portrayal as an alienated being is no accident. She is but one of several such characters in *The Snow Queen*. Equally estranged are Sparks, Moon's cousin and lover; Jerusha, a highly capable but emotionally tortured police inspector; BZ Gundhalinu, Jerusha's pride-ridden and rigidly structured aide; and Arienrhod, the beautiful but power-crazed Winter Queen. Moreover, these characters reflect a pattern that predominates in Vinge's writing. Most of her major works contain at least one alienated character, usually the protagonist. There are, for example, Betha Torgussen and Wadie Abdhiamal of *The Outcasts of Heaven Belt*, Mythili Fukinuki and Chaim Dartagnan of "Legacy," Amanda Montoya and Cristoval Hoffmann of "Phoenix in the Ashes," Etaa of "Mother and Child," T'uupieh of "Eyes of Amber," and Tarawassie and Moon Shadow of "The Crystal Ship."

To find alienation the major theme of Vinge's writing is no surprise, for as critic Blanche Gelfant has indicated, it "is the inextricable theme of modern American fiction." Indeed, it may well be the major theme of modern world fiction, for in addition to notable American writers like Theodore Dreiser, Ernest Hemingway, John Dos Passos, and Saul Bellow, it is also the primary subject of such foreign writers as Jean-Paul Sartre, Albert Camus, Andre Malraux, Franz Kafka, and Herman Hesse, and as a literary form, it can be traced back directly to Fyodor Dostoevsky's *Notes from the Underground*. While the characteristics of the alienated human have existed independently for centuries, their crystallization into a major phenomenon is primarily the result of the events of the last century: rapid industrialization, global wars, deterioration of the cities, pollution of the environment, dilution of culture, dehumanization of art, refinement of the establishment, mass anaesthetization of humans, and so on. Regardless of the causes, however, the result has been to create societies that are maladjusted and comprised of individuals who accept these maladjustments as normal without realizing that they will eventually find themselves alienated from them without knowing why.

Since the term alienation was first introduced into English with the publication of Erich Fromm's *Marx's Concept of Man*, it has been so overused that its meaning is often unclear. It may be defined metaphysically, for example, as G.W.F. Hegel does, or psychologically as Ludwig Feuerbach does, or economically as Karl Marx does. Despite this breadth of concept and its subsequent dilution, however, all the definitions have a common ground best set forth perhaps by F. H. Heinemann:

> The facts to which the term "alienation" refer, are, objectively different kinds of disassociation, break or rupture between human beings and their objects, whether the latter be other persons, or the natural world, or their own creations in art, science and society; and subjectively, the corresponding states of disequilibrium, disturbance, strangeness and anxiety. . . . There is one point common to all of them, i.e., the belief that a preceding unity and harmony has been transformed into disunity and disharmony.

And, the psychological characteristics of an alienated person can be identified. In describing the "Underground Man," a neurotic extension of the alienated man, Edward Abood lists the following. (1) He is usually at odds with the prevailing norms of the society in which he lives and the forces that perpetuate it. This animosity may extend to Nature, Being, or God. (2) He may either be in active revolt against the society, or he may have turned in upon himself with such ferocity that he has been reduced to despair and a longing for death. (3) His commitments are subjective, and thus he is isolated and estranged. (4) Emotionally, he is lonely, frustrated, anxious, and tense. Sometimes, this is aggravated by a keen, often morbid sensibility. (5) His attitude is typically negative. If he does develop a positive philosophy, it begins with and is conditioned by a denial of the codes of conduct, especially the values, by which those in his culture live. To these we can add the feeling of being manipulated, used, or exploited, a characteristic identified by Marx and several psychologists. Taken together, these qualities comprise the prototype of an individual alienated to the point of being psychotic. It is important to remember, however, that there are differences of degree involved. Not all alienated individuals will display all the qualities that comprise the prototype, nor will they suffer them severely enough to be classified psychotic.

While being alienated certainly implies being neurotic, it does not inevitably spell psychological disaster. Some individuals do struggle and fail in their attempts to cope with their cultures. Others succeed. The latter group first began to appear in American fiction at the end of the 1960s when many authors started producing works in which the protagonists transcend their conditions: loneliness, estrangement from the world and from self. Inevitably, success is impelled by love, for it is characters who love themselves, another, and the world who do transcend. Abood confirms that alienation need not be fatal when he points out that Camus, Sartre, and Malraux all use the condition as a foundation for constructing new and positive value systems that permit their characters to reach some reconciliation with their cultures. The belief that man can transcend his alienation is held by several philosophers and psychologists, who have been termed "utopian existentialists." While accepting that estrangement is a condition of present-day society, they believe that it can be overcome by future sociological and psychological developments.

Among this group, psychologist Erich Fromm, in particular, believes that transcendence is possible. He sees alienation as evolutionary. "Human nature drives toward unity with the 'all,' with nature; but unity on the highest level requires a temporary separation, and consequent loneliness. One goes out in order to return enriched. Separation, though painful, is a progressive step." To accomplish the transcendence, man must establish a sense of identity based upon his experience of self as the subject and agent of his own powers. This will occur when he grasps reality both inside and outside himself. Transcendence is characterized by a productive orientation in which the ability to love and create is predominant.

Though there is no evidence that Vinge has consciously based her characters in Fromm's psychology, the fact is that they closely parallel his thinking. They exhibit the qualities of alienated individuals. Then, by virtue of their experiences, they form new value systems and manage to transcend their estrangement. They do this by learning to love, and they learn to love by learning to communicate. In maturing, some of them even develop the potential to change their cultures. A close examination of Vinge's stories will demonstrate this pattern.

Mythili Fukinuki and Chaim Dartagnan of "Legacy" both exhibit characteristics of alienation. They are at odds with the norms of their culture, they are lonely, tense, and frustrated. Chaim is a "media man," which forces him to survive by flattering the wealthy and powerful. It is a position of high esteem in the fragile Heaven Belt culture. Yet, his self-loathing produces such disgust in him that it is "transmuted into physical self-punishment" and his stomach "pays the price of too many false smiles." Still, he persists until the attempted murder of Mythili, whom he has come to care for, forces him to acknowledge his integrity and suffer the consequences of the action he must take to preserve it.

Mythili is equally at odds with her culture. She is a female spaceship pilot in a society that will not honorably permit its women any role other than childbearer. Moreover, she has voluntarily undergone sterility. She is resented both for her burning desire to succeed as a pilot and for choosing to eliminate her breeding capability when the Heaven Belt culture needs all the healthy children it can get to maintain its faltering technology. Steven Spruill writes: "She burns with inner integrity, a dedication to her *self* at the other extreme of Dartagnan's utter, if unintended, self-abnegation. By trying so hard to exist on her own terms, to resist the malicious pressures of maledom and the passive restricted example of her society's women, she courts paranoia and madness." Mythili's breech of Heaven Belt values is an active revolt against them. Dartagnan, on the other hand, has turned in on himself with such ferocity that he has been reduced nearly to despair. The commitments of both characters are subjective and their attitudes negative.

Both are also frustrated and lonely. This is most evident in the scene where they are just completing the exploration of a planetoid in the Main Belt. It had promised salvagable goods, but all they found were masses of old printouts and plastic packing crates and a pair of mummified bodies. Disappointed, Chaim returns to their ship and once inside begins to retch, a reaction to his ulcer. Concerned, Mythili follows and in the exchange that follows, he compares himself to "those crazy bastards down in the rock, drowning in garbage, dying by centimeters—just like this goddamned system!"

She suggests that they are not at all like that reclusive couple they found. He counters that they are worse because they had a chance to be something more, hinting of course that they could be lovers. She rejects the idea angrily. She still cannot forgive him for suggesting to Demarch Siamang, a man who tried to kill her because she was unwilling to help him cover up a murder he committed, that he abandon her on the surface of a hostile planet even though she knows that Chaim's suggestion was the only way to save her life. Defeated and frustrated, he replies, "Get the hell out of here, then. Let me be alone by myself." Other evidence of Dartagnan's loneliness is found earlier in the story. His relationship with Mythili seems very promising, and it suddenly occurs to him that the reason he has always hated prospecting was because of its loneliness. A moment later a book of poems falls open in his hands to a page where Mythili has written: "*It will be lonely to be dead; but it cannot be much more lonely than it is to be alive!*" Next to her plain, back-slanted writing, he pens, "Yes, yes, yes."

Moon Shadow and Tarawassie of "The Crystal Ship" suffer the same characteristics of alienation that Dartagnan and Mythili do. They are at odds with the norms of their society, lonely, frustrated, and tense. Moon Shadow, a kangaroolike creature, is initially divorced from his own kind, called the Real People, because he is the last offspring produced by the mating of one of his own kind and one of the humans who came to colonize his planet. He has been ostracized from his kith because he insists upon trying to teach his people that change offered through the superior technology of the humans is preferable to their current stagnation. But they want no part of it. They remember too vividly how they were decimated and exploited by the humans. Moon Shadow, on the other hand, cannot help trying to teach them, for he is a repository for the memories of all his ancestors, and a special organ inside his pouch permits him to draw an outside mind into his own and down into his racial consciousness. Nonetheless, his compulsion to teach the ways of the humans is an active breach of Real People values. He has been hounded into a solitary, half-fugitive existence, spied on and abused, and denied the rituals of the clan.

Tarawassie, a young girl who lives in a starship orbiting high above the planet, is equally alienated. Like most of the other remaining humans, she is completely removed from reality, living initially only for the highs induced by *chitta*, a native drug that when introduced to the colonists five hundred years earlier caused the society to collapse. Happy and unaware at first, the deaths of a friend and then her mother stir her curiosity to wakefulness. Both committed suicide in the mysterious Star Well of the ship. When no one can satisfactorily explain what the Star Well is and why she has begun to have nightmares, she seeks an answer in the ruined city below because that is where Andar, her dead friend, had found it.

When she becomes lost in the city and cut off from any chitta, her long-suppressed emotions begin to take over, and she is overwhelmed by loneliness. As she continues to withdraw from the drug, she encounters Fromm's reality both inside and outside herself:

> She remembered the sight of her own starved body, the reflection of a terrible truth. Because it was true, she was certain of it now. The self and the reality that she had always known had been a dream, a dream. But not a fantasy. She remembered her mother's death, the Star Well. Were this ruined world and her own wretchedness what her mother had seen without chitta? And was this what Andar had seen?

Moon Shadow tries to help her find an answer, and in the process she learns to read. This only increases her divorce from her own kind. When at last she is fully aware of how the colony fell and the insufferable dead end that now presents itself as her future, she thinks: "But even knowing that they [she and Moon Shadow] were valued by one another, she knew that they would both always feel isolated, alienated, lost, because they had no purpose here, no reason for existing in an alien world." Passive at first, Tarawassie actively revolts against her system's values and eventually steps into the Star Well to escape her living death. The Star Well, she believes, is a transporter that can create duplicate bodies at its terminus on Earth, and when Tarawassie steps into it she performs the ultimate rejection of her society's values.

Perhaps the purest and most direct example of a character at odds with the norms of her society, lonely, tense, and frustrated occurs in Amanda Montoya of "Phoenix in the Ashes." Like Moon Shadow she too has been ostracized. She chose love over a marriage arranged by her father, but when the sailor she promised to wait for fails to return, she is forced from her father's home and her dowry is distributed between her two sisters. Now she lives in an adobe cottage on her father's land but far from the main house, and gleans his fields for food. Though he refuses to acknowledge her existence, he has not so completely forgotten her that he would force her to become a beggar or a whore, the only occupations left to a woman of San Pedro who has lost her family sponsorship. In this rigid, male-dominated society, women are regarded as valuable property. From birth they are impressed with the need for obedience and chastity; their role is to serve their husbands and fathers blindly. They weave and cook but do not read.

Amanda's rebellion costs her dearly. Even though other pockets of civilization remain in this postbomb world, San Pedro maintains only limited trading relationships. Because of religious stringency, leaving the society is nearly impossible. So, eight years after her rebellion, Amanda survives at a minimum level. She is bitter, she is lonely, and she finds that "the staid ritual life in San Pedro [is] suffocating her, and her dreams [are] dying."

Amanda's rebellion extends beyond the defiance of her father. She rebels in fact against her God when she gives refuge to Cristoval Hoffmann, a prospector whose helicopter crashed into her father's field. Believing him to have been struck from the sky by God because he was an agent of evil, the villagers invoke their "Angel of the Prophet" to ward off any powers he might have and leave him to die. Amanda explains to him later that the villagers thought that by flying he was performing sorcery. He asks if she were not afraid of God's punishment for helping him, and she replies, "There's little more that God could do to me or I to God. . . ."

Hoffmann, a prospector of rare scrap metals for the Brazilian government, is as alienated as Amanda. He enjoys his profession because it takes him away from the greed and exploitation of his own society. During the exchange when Cohelo, his boss, asks him to take the assignment that brings him eventually to San Pedro, he says, "I use you, you use me. . . ." When Hoffmann crashes, his alienation is increased twofold because he not only loses his only means of returning to Brazil but also suffers amnesia, which prevents him from even remembering his previous life.

If Vinge's characters are not at odds with their own societies, they are at odds within the societies they find themselves and are alienated from them. This displacement occurs, for example, to Etaa, the Kotaane priestess of the powerful novelette "Mother and Child." While she never loses faith with her own native Nature cult, Etaa is twice removed from it physically. First, she is kidnapped by Meron, King of Tramaine. Then, she is kidnapped from Tramaine by Wic'owoyake, one of the silicon-based life forms believed to be gods by Meron and his people. Nicknamed Tam by Etaa, Wic'owoyake actually removes her from her home, a moon circling a giant, gaseous planet called Cyclops, to Laa Merth, another moon now uninhabited. Physical displacement and isolation are, of course, symbols of alienation, but there are other signs as well. Believed to be a witch and too uncouth to be a consort of the King, Etaa is rejected by the Tramanians. Her rape by Meron speeds her withdrawal and virtually eliminates all communication with him, but her disgust with the Tramanians is more fundamental. She believes them to be pitiful and cursed because they do not believe in the Earth-Mother goddess that dominates her religion.

When Tam removes her to Laa Merth for political reasons, Etaa withdraws even farther. Not only does she cease virtually all communications with Tam, she never ventures outside their shelter again by choice. Though estranged, manipulated by an outside source, and literally isolated, Etaa never falls into despair. She has Alfilere, her infant son, to think about and to care for. His welfare prevents her from becoming completely subjective, and more importantly he is a symbol of her love for Hywel, her husband. That her love for him still lives is confirmed by the fact that she kept the silver-bell earring he gave her close to her during her entire ordeal even though she believed him to be dead.

Betha Torgussen of *The Outcasts of Heaven Belt* is yet another character displaced from her own society. Even though her displacement is voluntary, she cannot easily or quickly return to her home planet of Morningside, for it is three light-years away. Betha and six other members of her extended family form the crew of the starship *Ranger*, whose mission it is to establish trading arrangements with the Heaven Belt worlds. They believe those worlds to be rich in metals and frozen gases, commodities that will improve their own bleak existence.

But an unprovoked attack by chemically-powered rockets from the Grand Harmony of the Discan Rings, one of the two major groups remaining after a devastating civil war, kills five of the *Ranger*'s crew. Their deaths ravage Betha emotionally:

> He was gone; they were gone: her crew, her family . . . her husbands and her wives. Her strength, the strength that comes from sharing, was gone with them, bled away into the bottomless void. How would she go on? Loss was too heavy a burden, to bear alone. . . .

Later in the story, another event serves to alienate her further. As she and other crew members are attempting to lash much needed cylinders of hydrogen to the hull of the *Ranger*, a loose cable hits her in the chest and throws her out into space. Suddenly alone, injured, and spinning free in the dark immensity of space, Betha has both literally and symbolically taken another step toward estrangement.

Her rejection of Heaven Belt values is born from her disappointment. She finds the system to be a trap, a betrayal because it promised a life of ease and luxury, but instead it damned human weakness without pity. The Demarchy, in particular, symbolizes her frustration:

> She cursed the Demarchy, the obsessive veneer of sophistication, the artificial gaiety, the pointless waste of their media broadcasts. Fools, reveling in their fanatical independence when they should all be working together; living on self-serving self-sufficiency, with no stable government to control them, no honest bonds of kinship, but only the equal selfishness of every other citizen. . . . And their women, useless, frivolous, gaudy, the ultimate waste in a society that desperately needed every resource, including its human resources.

Though hunted by both the Demarchy and the Grand Harmony and though wounded by her deep loneliness, she remains actively in revolt against the values of the system. Though frustrated, tense, and anxious, her commitments never become subjective. And though her attitude is decidedly negative, her sense of responsibility never permits her to despair.

Wadie Abdhiamal, a negotiator for the Demarchy, is equally alienated. By his own admission, his private life is barren of any real relationships. He feels the loneliness but manages to minimize its effects by submerging himself in his job until his contact with Betha and the circumstances surrounding the *Ranger* itself force him to confront himself. One of the events that makes his alienation painfully aware to him occurs when he is declared a traitor and sentenced to death *in absentia*. After a run-in with a merchant who wants the ship for himself, Wadie boards the *Ranger* to continue to negotiate its use for the Demarchy. Unfortunately, the merchant fabricates a story that clearly shows Wadie to be a traitor and tells his boss and the media. Wadie, who is offered a chance to respond electronically to the charges, rejects it to protect the location of the ship. Since he does not answer the charges, however, he is presumed guilty.

When Wadie later uses his position to help the *Ranger* blackmail hydrogen from the Ringers, he eliminates his last hope for refuge in the system and finds himself completely isolated. Betha describes him as "a man with no family . . . and now no friends, no world, no future." Full realization of his alienation comes to him as he leaps off into space to save Betha after she is struck by the cable. "The immensity of isolation stifled him, filling the black-and-brilliant desolation like sand, dragging at him, holding him back . . . as the isolation of his own making had cut him off from truth all his life."

"Eyes of Amber," Vinge's Hugo Award winning novella, presents an interesting variation of the alienation theme. T'uupieh the protagonist, is an excellent example of what Erich Fromm calls "socially patterned defect." As a female assassin among the winged creatures of Saturn's moon, Titan, she accepts the values of her culture, at least at the conscious level, even though her people are treacherous, devious, dangerous, unethical, and immoral by our standards. T'uupieh not only embraces those values but, in fact, promotes them. When she is dispossessed of her lands by the Overlord and is forced to live by her wits, for example, she resolves to become the best thief and cutthroat in the land. She succeeds amazingly well until a space probe introduces her indirectly to Shannon Wyler, an ex-rock musician with a facility for computers. T'uupieh is an excellent example of a person who has learned "to live with a defect without becoming ill" because her culture provides patterns that act as opiates.

The acceptance of Titan's values does not, however, prevent T'uupieh from becoming alienated and lonely. The loss of her lands and her wealth brings a radical change in her life-style and a subsequent loss of prestige and security. The marriage of her sister, Ahtseet, to the man who stole their lands and property, eliminates her closest companion and confidante. Her subsequent rise to leadership of a band of outcasts like herself forces her to maintain her distance from them in order to control them. And, when she finds the probe, it only serves to alienate her further:

> She looked away again, toward the fire, toward the cloak-wrapped form of her outlaws. Since the demon had come to her she had felt both the physical and emotional space that she had always kept between herself as leader and her band of followers gradually widening. She was still completely their leader, perhaps more firmly so because she had tamed the demon, and their bond of shared danger and mutual respect had never weakened. But there were other needs, which her people might fill for each other, but never for her.

The more she relies on the probe, her demon, the greater her degree of alienation will become, for Shannon is weaning her from her values and toward ours. The process is aided by her perception of the probe as a supernatural thing. Her reaction is greatly influenced by her fear and awe of its powers.

T'uupieh is neither despairing nor longing for death. Her commitments are selfish, at least up until the time she is forced to admit to herself that her sister's escape from death pleased her. In fact, despite the loneliness, she feels good about herself. She is successful, but she does not realize that her feeling occurs because defect has been raised to a virtue by her culture.

From these illustrations, it is clear that alienation is a major component of Vinge's characterization. It does produce withdrawal from one's own kind, rebellion against a society's values, loneliness (the affective corollary of alienation), tension, anxiety, frustration, even physical illness, but it is not an irreversible condition like Sören Kierkegaard's "sickness unto death." Rather, it is evolutionary. It is a stage a personality must pass through on its way to transcendence. From this point of view, it parallels Erich Fromm's position and is much like what an adolescent passes through in his search for identity.

For Vinge alienation is the result of the compelling drive of her characters toward the realization of their potentials. Completing their quests for fulfillment brings them into conflict with the values of the societies in which they find themselves because the societies themselves are neurotic and unrealized. Yet, Vinge's characters escape their alienation with both dignity and integrity because they persevere in their attempts to grasp reality, both inside and outside themselves. They continue to strive to understand themselves, to align themselves with nature, and to communicate with all things, especially in emotional terms. Moon realizes this as she tries to make friends with Blodwed's caged pets in *The Snow Queen*. "She lost track of time or any purpose beyond the need to communicate even to the smallest degree with every creature, and earn for herself the reward of its embryonic trust. . . ." Like Moon, Vinge's other characters also succeed in achieving something like Fromm's "productive orientation characterized by the ability to love and create." For Vinge, communication and love are psychologically opposed to alienation and loneliness.

Because love is the ultimate communication, and communication, in the broadest and deepest sense of the word, is the means for breaking down alienation, Vinge frequently focuses her stories on love relationships. In particular, she brings together an alienated man and an alienated woman and lets them work at communicating. Bound together by their loneliness and prompted by the events of the story that continuously force them together, they eventually break down the barriers between them and achieve a love relationship based upon mutual trust. Their common enemy is often the values of the society in which they find themselves. From the exertion of their mutual struggle, they forge new value systems and come to a more complete realization of their own potentials. Battling to survive at both the physical and psychological levels, they do produce or promise to produce changes in the value system of the society itself.

Such is the case in "Legacy." Mythili and Chaim are both alienated. When he is chosen as media man and she as pilot of Sabu Siamang's rescue mission to Planet Two, a sequence of events forces them not only to communicate with but to trust one another. When Siamang kills Sekka-Olefin, the prospector he is supposed to be rescuing, for the computer software he controls and subsequently tries to cover up the crime, both Mythili and Chaim are forced to recognize the fact that the values of their society are not only undesirable but psychologically unhealthy. Mythili's refusal to cover up the crime forces Siamang to try to kill her. The incident makes Chaim aware of the limits of his own integrity and forces him to make a realistic choice in order to save them both: he convinces Siamang to abandon Mythili on the planet's surface rather than "spacing" her on the way home. He argues that she will either freeze or suffocate if they jam the oxygen valve on her suit. Either way, her death will look like an accident. But Dartagnan knows something that neither Mythili nor the drug-crazed Siamang knows—the air of Planet Two is breathable, at least for a short time. Olefin told him that when Siamang was out of the shelter. Chaim's choice is difficult but realistic. He also knows that Mythili can make it back to Olefin's shelter and fix his landing module, if she does not panic. Under the existing conditions, it is the best possible decision. When they finally land on Mecca, their home asteroid, Dartagnan publicly charges Siamang with the murder, knowing full well that he may also be charged with Mythili's death if she fails to escape. She does escape, however, and he ruins his career as a media man, but he has learned something valuable about himself and his world. So has she. Subsequent situations force greater understanding, eventually permitting them to build new, more healthy value systems and to fall in love.

The pattern recurs in "The Crystal Ship." Impelled by her desire to understand the Star Well, Tarawassie is forced to rely upon Moon Shadow. After an accidental meeting, she learns that he can help her to understand the terrible conditions of their society. In learning of the reality surrounding her, however, she increases her alienation from the remaining humans on the Crystal Ship. Through Moon Shadow's ability to draw her into his mind and thus allow her to become the ancestors who inhabit it, she not only learns the truth but experiences a schizophrenia similar to what Moon experiences when she invades the mind of Fate Ravenglass. While it is a symbol of alienation, it is also means for Tarawassie to develop a deep understanding of both Moon Shadow and humans who are not addicted to chitta. Their relationship, on the other hand, alleviates his loneliness. A genuine affection develops between them, one based in reality and in the new value systems each forms.

In "Phoenix in the Ashes," the pattern occurs again. When Hoffmann's 'copter crashes in Amanda's father's field, events are set in motion that make Amanda and Cristoval communicate with and rely upon one another. He needs her to nurse him back to health; she needs him to reaffirm her independence and integrity. Their continuous reliance upon one another forges a relationship based upon values different from San Pedro's and brings both of them a new perception of reality. Eventually they marry, and Amanda learns that a realistic love relationship is very different from the romance she sought with the sailor who abandoned her.

The pattern is varied somewhat in "Mother and Child." Etaa's psychological journey is cyclical: from love and communication through alienation and loneliness and back to love again. But the love she feels by the end of her journey is much different than what she felt at the beginning. It is a love based in maturity and reality rather than one based in innocence. It is broader, deeper, and wiser. Events again force her to rely on alienated individuals: Hywel, her husband; Meron, the King of Tramaine; and Tam, the shape-changing, alien, xenobiologist. Each of them is initially alienated and lonely, but their experiences with her change them. Each achieves a new perception of reality, new understanding, and new value systems because they learn to love her.

She too is changed by her ordeal. Believing Hywel to be dead, Etaa finds solace in her responsibility to her infant son. But she is forced to rely first on Meron and then on Tam for her physical survival. She grows from her experiences with them. She matures; she broadens her understanding of reality; she forms new values:

"I am not what I was. And neither is the world." Her hands dropped; her eyes found my face again. "One's truth is another's lie, Tam; how can we say what is right, when it's always changing? We only know what we feel . . . that's all we ever know."

The Outcasts of Heaven Belt treats the pattern in a more conventional way. Betha Torgussen is very lonely after five members of her extended family are killed. When Wadie Abdhiamal is assigned to negotiate the use of Betha's ship, the *Ranger*, for the Demarchy, events are set in motion that force them to communicate, and this both expands their understanding of one another and forges a bond between them. Wadie uses his position as Negotiator, for example, to help Betha and the others blackmail hydrogen from the Ringers, and he saves her life. She provides him refuge from a system that has condemned him to death as a traitor. Both learn that Heaven is not what it was promised to be, and their relationship helps them to form new values. By breaking down the barriers between them, they develop a creative relationship based on trust, communication, and new, more realistic perceptions.

"Eyes of Amber" presents yet another variation on the pattern. While both T'uupieh and Shannon Wyler are alienated and lonely, there is never any physical contact between them. In fact, T'uupieh is not even aware that she is in contact with another intelligent being. In her highly superstitious society, she believes the probe through which they communicate to be a demon. It brings her power, so she relies on it more and more to accomplish her ends. In the process, however, she becomes more and more alienated from her own kind. Because the probe is animated, she develops a relationship with it analogous to love. In replying to a question from one of her band at the end of the story, for instance, she says, "'The Wheel of Change carries us all, but not with equal ease. Is that not so, my beautiful Shang'ang [her name for the probe].' She stroked its day-warmed carapace tenderly, and settled down on the softening ground to wait for its reply." Communication between T'uupieh and the probe has eased her loneliness and altered her values. While she has begun to accept Wyler's values, he has learned that communication can indeed make a difference. He did prevent T'uupieh from murdering her sister. In the process, he has reached an understanding with his mother that promises to alleviate his own alienation from her.

The Snow Queen presents an even more complicated variation on the pattern. It is similar to "Mother and Child" in that it moves cyclically, from innocent love through alienation to mature love, and it involves more than one other alienated individual. As the novel begins, Moon and Sparks are naively happy, but when they both seek acceptance as sibyls and Sparks is rejected, he leaves his warm, southern homeland for Carbuncle, the capital, in the north. As Moon's selection for training overtly marks the beginning of her alienation (she is unaware that the very nature of her birth has already marked her), Sparks's rejection marks his alienation. Instead of being forced together to learn to understand each other, themselves, nature, God, and their people, they are torn apart. Reality is thrust upon them through their experiences and relationships with the outside world. Into the mix, Vinge inserts Arienrhod, the Winter Queen. She is Moon's mother, by cloning, though the two do not know one another, and she is Moon's mirror image: evil, insensitive, power mad, and accomplished in the ways of the world.

As events unfold, Arienrhod permits Starbuck, her right hand and lover, to be ousted by Sparks and then takes him as lover. The relationship is logical. Arienrhod possesses the secret of longevity, so age is not a factor, and as Moon's genetic equivalent, she bears the physical and mental characteristics that attracted Sparks to Moon in the first place. But her power over Sparks is so complete that she corrupts him, and as he becomes more dependent upon her, his alienation deepens.

The relationship among Moon, Sparks, and Arienrhod is broadly defined by Hans Christian Andersen's fairy tale, also entitled "The Snow Queen" and one of the novel's sources. In Andersen's story, Kay, a young boy, is struck in the eye and the heart by slivers from a magic mirror invented by a wicked hobgoblin and then shattered. The mirror's power is to distort all that is beautiful and to turn the heart cold. Kay wanders off to live with the Snow Queen, oblivious to the cares and concerns of Gerda, a young girl who loves him. She is persistent, and she learns what is wrong with him, finds him, and heals him with a kiss whose power is drawn from her innocence.

Moon's psychological journey, however, is not that simple. While Sparks is writhing uncomfortably in the clutches of Arienrhod, she must first solve the problem of her own alienation. Her destiny is not her own; she is manipulated by the Old Empire computer, which places her inevitably into conflict with the values of both the Winters and the Summers. While she is trying to realize her personality, she is also gaining experience that broadens her perception of reality. Though she bears the same genetic program as Arienrhod, environment has shaped her differently.

In the other stories, communication between the alienated female and the alienated male mutually brought them to a better understanding of reality and fostered new value systems that brought love, but in *The Snow Queen* it is Moon who must force the personality transcendences. Not until she finally locates Sparks and sleeps with him is he even aware that he is under some kind of "spell." Only then, and after his father has acknowledged his parentage, is Sparks's alienation resolved. In a conversation with Moon about the pledge they made to always love one another but subsequently broke, Sparks dismisses his need for a festival mask by saying, "No . . . I don't need one. I've already taken mine off." His literal reference is to the mask he was required to wear as Starbuck, but his symbolic reference is to the persona he has shed in casting off his alienation.

While the pattern of an alienated woman forced through a series of experiences with an alienated man expresses Vinge's concern for communication, the enlarged perception of reality that each character aquires also brings a benefit with it. It is that each transcended protagonist finds herself with the ability to change the values of her society or the promise to do so. As the Summer Queen, for example, Moon will integrate the values of the Winter and Summer peoples and through the power of the sibyl computer, will begin to recreate the Old Empire civilization on Tiamat. Where Arienrhod has failed because of her insensitivity and alienation, Moon will succeed because of her ability to love in a psychologically healthy way. With the power of the probe, T'uupieh possesses the capability to change her culture's values. With the fusion reactor engine of the *Ranger*, Betha possesses a tool to teach the Heaven Belt peoples the value of cooperation. Because of her unique relationship with Tam and the belief that her son is the heir to the Tramaine throne, Etaa possesses the means to change not only the societies of her own world but also those of the aliens. Amanda's

rebellion has brought San Pedro Hoffmann's knowledge of crop rotation and the promise of a more productive agriculture. And though
not made clear until Vinge wrote the "Afterword" to the story, Tarawassie and Moon Shadow do eventually set in motion the forces that
will bring understanding to both the humans and the Real People of
their world.

In order to frame the fight her characters must wage against the
values of the various societies in which they find themselves, Vinge
usually sets her stories in worlds that are either very primitive or have
been destroyed by some disaster. This permits her to create societies
that have values that are obviously unhealthy and that suffer from
Fromm's socially patterned defect. The distopic worlds, where created
by technology, also suggest the dangers of human folly.

"Legacy" and *The Outcasts of Heaven Belt*, for example, are set in an
asteroid system whose civilizations have been virtually destroyed by
a civil war that killed a hundred million people. What remains are
fragile societies slowly disintegrating into chaos. Natural resources are
scarce. Radiation has produced sterility and a high number of cripples.
The will to survive has given preeminence to greed and selfishness.
The Demarchy is marked by lying, cheating, distrust, convenience,
and suffering. People must scavenge to live. Women are valued only
for their fertility. Cooperation has been replaced by division. It is a
society that is psychologically unhealthy and one that easily breeds
estrangement.

The planet upon which Tarawassie and Moon Shadow live, in "The
Crystal Ship," contains the remains of a society destroyed by drugs.
Its population has been depleted of both humans and Real People. Its
cities are crumbling, its machines lie rusting, its libraries gather dust,
its people are starving. Fear and superstition prevail. Progress is ig-
nored. Technology is distrusted. Even the purposes of the books and
machines have been forgotten by all but a few, and the humans, who
do apathetically survive, dream away their lives in drug-induced
trances, some of them in the beautiful crystal ship that orbits endlessly
above the pinwheel-clouded world. The Real People have returned to
the ways of the past and reject any suggestion of progress, regardless
of how difficult living may become. Because it is a world whose peoples
refuse to recognize reality, it is a world that promotes alienation.

The setting for "Phoenix in the Ashes" is Earth of the future, dev-
astated by an atomic holocaust that has left isolated pockets of civili-

zation. The San Pedro group, to which Amanda Montoya belongs, is primitive and fundamentalistic. Wrapped in religious superstition, it values its women only as servants to its men. Agriculture dominates, technology is feared, contact with other surviving cultures is limited because of distrust. Morality is strictly regulated. It is a rigid and conservative culture that suppresses personal development except through prescribed and narrow channels.

The world of "Mother and Child" has been ravaged by a plague that left most of its people either infertile or crippled by mutations. Vision and hearing, in particular, have been severely affected. The two principal societies of the world have developed along lines dictated by these impairments. Their religions especially reflect them. People with perfect vision, for example, are said to have "second sight" and become priestesses among the Kotaane. On the other hand, the church of the Neaane believes hearing to be a curse and punctures the eardrums of any child born with that ability. Rather than working toward some reconciliation beneficial to both societies, however, the Kotaane and the Neaane have developed a deep distrust of one another. Their cultural stagnation has been encouraged by the shape-changing aliens, thought to be gods by the Neaane because they fear the potential destructiveness of humans. While living in primitive harmony with Nature is the principal concern of the Kotaane culture, the Neaane's concerns are more material. Both groups are ignorant of their true situations. Therefore, their values breed an unhealthy psychology and eventual alienation.

Though no specific cause is given, the Titanian civilization of "Eyes of Amber" is also distopic. It is primitive compared to Earth, with knowledge of even the basest technology almost nonexistent. Fear and superstition dominate. Murder, thievery, deceit, and other acts regarded as sins on Earth are held in high regard. Indeed, the better one practices these vices, the better one's chances of surviving, and survival is the ultimate goal of Titan's population. Greed, selfishness, and distrust are the dominant values of this society and the enemies of psychologically healthy communication. So, alienation and loneliness are inevitable. Since the Titanians know nothing else, they learn to live with it.

The world of *The Snow Queen* also encourages alienation and loneliness. Tiamat is a planet entering a 150-year period during which it will be totally isolated from the other civilized worlds comprising the

Hegemony. About to withdraw from Tiamat, Hegemony officials plan to take with them the secrets of the technology they refuse to share with the natives. The planet will revert to a very primitive level under the control of the Summers who will rule it during its isolated phase. Under the leadership of the Winters and Queen Arienrhod, society has developed negatively. Vice, distrust, and insensitivity dominate. But Tiamat is not alone in its alienation. All the worlds of the Hegemony are in a postdestructive period. A higher culture prevailed when the Old Empire was intact, but it was destroyed in a devastating civil war. Though measures were taken to assure a rapid return from the "dark ages" that were sure to follow, recovery has been very slow.

Vinge's distopic worlds also serve another purpose. They represent and support the winter season in the death and revival of vegetation archetype that she uses as a broad metaphor to symbolize the psychological development of her characters. Simply stated, the winter period, or death phase of vegetation, is equivalent to the alienation of the characters. The revival of vegetation in the spring is equivalent to the personality transcendence of the characters. The distopic worlds are the "waste land" or "wounded land" of the Grail Quest myths. In those myths, the "wounded land" (it is either suffering from drought or infertility, though it may indeed be wounded in other ways) is connected with the illness of the Fisher King, and the task of the hero is to cure both the land and the King. This is not to suggest that Vinge is writing Grail Quest stories. It is simply to point out a device that she uses to emphasize the psychological condition of her characters, who, since they are suffering from alienation and loneliness, are ill and must be cured.

While it occurs in a number of variations, the death and revival of vegetation story occurs in many of the world's mythologies. It is a personification of the fate of most vegetation during the changing seasons. It blooms in the spring, thrives through the summer, and dies in the fall only to be reborn the following spring. During the winter, of course, the land is dormant. Of particular interest to agrarian cultures, who literally survived on a single crop, the natural pattern was converted into a drama with supernatural overtones because the process was beyond the knowledge of the culture and thus seemed to be magic. In its most primitive form, the King or Queen of vegetation dies, or is sacrificed, and enters the nether world. Then, through the intervention of another god or goddess, a mother, a sister, or a paramour, the god is induced to return to the surface. When he does, of course, the vegetation is revived. In a more general sense, the god's powers include all the reproductive energies of nature, and thus he may be considered the embodiment of the life principle itself. The Greek myth of Proserpine is illustrative of the archetype. She is carried off to the nether world by Pluto, and when her mother, Ceres, finds her gone, she blames the land, which is immediately struck barren. Upon discovering where her daughter is, Ceres implores Jupiter to return her daughter to her. He agrees to do so upon the condition that Proserpine must not have eaten any food while she was captive. She had tasted a pomegranate, however, so she cannot be completely released from Pluto's grasp. She is permitted to return to the surface to live with her mother for half a year in a compromise worked out by Jupiter. Ceres then removes her curse from the land, which is healed.

While the archetype is clearly present in all the stories being considered here, it is most obvious in *The Snow Queen*. In that novel, Vinge stresses that "the Change" is coming, that time when the Summers will ascend the throne of Tiamat after ritualistically destroying the Winter Queen and her consort. Quite imaginatively, after she is destroyed, the Vegetation Queen returns in the person of Moon, Arienrhod's clone, and with her comes the promise of revived vegetation. In the novel, Moon's presence promises the return of the reproductive energies of Nature as well as the revival of Old Empire culture and technology.

While several other symbols, devices, and motifs support this archetype, among the most important of them is Vinge's use of what Robert Graves has identified in his book of the same name as "The White Goddess." She is a goddess of the moon, most often portrayed as having three aspects: the New Moon, who is the white goddess of birth and growth; the Full Moon, who is the red goddess of love and battle; and the Old Moon, who is the black goddess of divination and death. As such, she goes through a cyclical process each month that results in renewal. It must be remembered, as Graves points out, that this Triple Goddess is the personification of primitive woman—"the creatress and destructress. As the New Moon or Spring, she was girl; as the Full Moon or Summer, she was woman; as the Old Moon or Winter, she was hag."

For each aspect of the White Goddess, Graves traces variations through many cultures. Most often, the three aspects are represented by the three mythical goddesses: Arianrhod, Blodeuwedd, and Cerridwen. Arianrhod is a Welsh goddess, who in the *Romance of Math the Son of Mathonwy* gives birth to a divine child. She then transforms into Blodeuwedd, a treacherous love goddess who destroys the divine child and then transforms again into a death goddess, known as the Old-Sow-Who-Eats-Her-Farrow, that is, her litter of pigs. In other words, she feeds on the flesh of the dead child. Not coincidentally, Arienrhod of *The Snow Queen* feeds symbolically off of Sparks. Like the divine child, Sparks is restored to life. Arianrhod, the Welsh goddess, was an orgiastic goddess whose worship included male sacrifices.

In Celtic legend, the third aspect (the Old Moon of death and divination) is Morgan le Fay, King Arthur's sister, a death goddess who often assumes the form of the raven. Morgan in Irish is "the Morrigan," meaning "Great Queen," and "le Faye" means "the fate." She was not the gentle figure depicted in *Morte d'Arthur* but rather she was more like "black, screaming hag, Cerridwen." From this analysis, of course, Vinge has constructed Fate Ravenglass, the gentle sibyl of the novel who chooses Moon to be queen. Moreover, she has also adopted and adapted other aspects of the "White Goddess." Arianrhod is loosely transformed into Arienrhod, Blodeuwedd becomes Blodwed, and Moon, who appears in the novel only as a young girl, obviously represents the New Moon, or the birth and regeneration, phase of the goddess. But even though Vinge has adopted their names, she has not necessarily paralleled her characters with the meanings attributed to them by myth. Arienrhod becomes both love goddess and death goddess in the novel, but she portrays love only in its most negative aspects. Blodwed, an illiterate and crude girl who tortures her pets in order to get them to obey her, performs only one important function in the book: she releases Moon in time for her to participate in the footrace that will determine the candidates for Summer Queen. While this is significant, her role hardly qualifies her for the reputation of her treacherous namesake.

There is one other characteristic of the "White Goddess" that is important to the novel. Cerridwen, the Old Moon aspect, is also known as the goddess of "Life-in-Death and Death-in-Life." She is the woman dicing with Death in Coleridge's *Ancient Mariner*. To be under her spell is to be in a "purgatory awaiting resurrection," and as Graves determines, that purgatory is in a "calm silver-circled castle at the back of the North Wind." All of Vinge's alienated characters are figuratively in a purgatory awaiting resurrection, and thus they are in a state of

"Death-in-Life." Tarawassie, for example, exists in such a state because of her chitta addiction, and Sparks is literally locked into such a state by the Winter Queen.

By its cyclical nature, its emphasis on growth and rebirth, and its reflection of the "Life-in-Death" state, the "White Goddess" motif clearly supports the death and revival of vegetation archetype.

Another supportive device is the fertility theme. It has obvious connections to the archetype because the death and subsequent revival of vegetation implies infertility and fertility, respectively. Except for "Eyes of Amber," where no particular emphasis is given to it other than the fact that Titan is just entering its spring season, all the stories place a premium on fertility. In "Mother and Child," for example, it is expressed through motherhood. The plague that struck the planet not only produced undesirable mutations but more importantly limited the ability of humans to reproduce. Lack of fertility thus gives birth a special emphasis. A respect for fertility is also apparent in the Kotaane religion, which makes "Mother Earth," and therefore "Mother Nature," its center and engages in a variety of fertility rituals.

In "Legacy" and *The Outcasts of Heaven Belt*, fertility is again conspicuous by its absence. Atomic spillage and the normal radiation from space have left most of the asteroid belt people either genetically defective, so that they fear to have children, or sterile. So concerned are they about their falling population (their failing technology requires a certain manpower level to maintain it), that they value their women almost exclusively for their ability to reproduce. Wadie Abdhiamal sums up the fate of a sterile woman in his society quite nicely when he says, she "had only two alternatives: to work at a menial, unpleasant job, exposed to radiation from the dirty postwar atomic batteries; or to work as a geisha, entertaining the clients of a corporation."

San Pedro, the primitive, agricultural village of "Phoenix in the Ashes," treats its women with equal defensiveness. Amanda Montoya's ostracism is an example of the punishment inflicted upon one who places herself outside the rigid mores of the community. Women are viewed as property, and their proper role is as servants to their fathers and husbands. They are expected to marry and raise families. The San Pedro religion is nature-centered. Their prophet, the son of God, who led them to the Los Angeles Basin from the south, revealed "that the only true and righteous life is one within the pattern of nature, the life all creatures were meant to live." And a seasonal cycle runs through the story. Hoffmann, who will increase their agricultural productivity by introducing them to crop rotation, comes to Amanda and the community from the field where he crashed while suffering from amnesia. Figuratively, he is reborn. Through the winter, he and Amanda lie fallow, and then in the spring they both bloom: "Amanda had blossomed with the spring, the ache of hunger forgotten. . . ." When Hoffmann's experiment at crop rotation produces wheat that grew taller than ever before, Amanda's father rewards him with the gift of a cow. Vinge leaves no doubt that the fertility images are to mirror the psychological development of her characters.

In *The Snow Queen*, fertility is treated more subtly. The shift of power to the Summers, after the ritual destruction of the Winter Queen, certainly suggests it since summer is the season of lush vegetation. But equally important is the symbolic value of Moon who becomes the Summer Queen and who is identified with the New Moon of the "White Goddess" symbol. It is the aspect of regeneration, growth, and rebirth. It is also important to note that Arienrhod is sterile. This is a side effect from taking the "waters of life," which though they extend life and suppress the effects of aging, do cause other problems. In "The Crystal Ship," there are no specific references to either fertility or motherhood, but fertility again becomes conspicuous by its absence. The preoccupation of the remaining human population with drugs has virtually ended all breeding, and from a simple lack of interest, the humans are now in danger of extinction.

In addition to the fertility theme, Vinge also uses a cluster of images suggesting coldness to support the dying and reviving vegetation archetype. Snow is the most prominent image, but also included in the cluster are ice and winter and adjectives like frozen and white, which suggest coldness. As a symbol, the cold cluster signifies the winter season, that season when the Earth is devoid of most vegetation. Psychologically, it signifies that period when the character is alienated and lonely. But, like winter it holds the promise of rebirth, renewal, and regeneration.

In "Mother and Child," for example, Hywel is orphaned near the end of winter, which marks the beginning of his alienation and loneliness, relieved only when he falls in love with Etaa, who as the priestess of the clan is the symbol of summer and fertility. When they are separated, it is at a cliff where "snow-water dashed itself down, down to oblivion." And Hywel, while relating the first part of the story, lies, his back broken in the leap from the cliff to escape King Meron's soldiers, in cold, drizzling rain under gray skies. Later, when Etaa is kidnapped by Tam and taken to Laa Merth, they arrive in a cold, gusting wind, and they spend the winter inside the shelter with virtually no communication between them. It is not until spring that a breakthrough comes.

In "Eyes of Amber" the spring melt is just beginning, and both the world and the characters are described in cold images. Chwiel compliments T'uupieh, for example, when he says, "You are carved from ice, T'uupieh," and later when she is speaking, Vinge describes her voice as one "which snapped like a frozen branch." Moreover, the frozen landscape of Titan stands in sharp contrast to the warm, interior scenes in the laboratory on Earth where Shannon Wyler works. The contrast marks the antithesis in values between the two cultures, and the cold images of Titan signify the alienation that exists in its people.

In "Legacy" and *The Outcasts of Heaven Belt*, the cold symbol takes a subtle and pervasive form. Integrated fully into the world of the stories, its primary manifestations are the near absolute cold of space and the "cold" fire of radiation. The people of Heaven Belt live inside asteroids with no atmospheres to protect them. Cold literally surrounds them as it surrounds the spaceships upon which most of the scenes of both stories are set. Vinge establishes the vastness and coldness of space as a symbol of alienation at the beginning of *The Outcasts of Heaven Belt* when she merges the icy images of Morningside's dark side with those of space and likens the *Ranger*'s flight to a moth drawn to the candleflame of the stars. But the cold symbol is also amplified by radiation, the heatless fire, which is everywhere in the system. Because of the failing technology, dampening screens no longer protect the people from it, either on the surface of the asteroids where many are forced to work or on their ships.

Snow does appear in both stories. In "Legacy," Planet Two, where Chaim, Mythili, and Siamang go to rescue Olefin, features snow and deep cold. Mythili is abandoned there and figuratively dies only to be reborn later from her alienation. The planet also offers hope for the Belters as a habitable world. In *The Outcasts of Heaven Belt*, the "Snows-of-Salvation" is a Ringer plant that processes snow into hydrogen and oxygen. Hydrogen is an important fuel. Snow itself, while symbolizing the alienation of the Belters, also holds out the promise of salvation.

The Snow Queen provides Vinge's most extensive use of the cold symbol. In addition to stacking the imagery, other more specific devices also support it: the ruling group of Tiamat at the time of the story is the Winters; events of the novel occur at the end of winter; one of the key sequences in Moon's development occurs when she is turned over to nomadic bandits by Sparks and held captive in the icebound highlands of the interior, which are rife with cold imagery. And Arienrhod, as the Snow Queen, is appropriately drawn as a cold figure. She is "an ethereal, pale sort, more to mind like her Edmund Dulac portrait; but she is also strong and relentless as ice. . . ." Psychologically, she parallels the Snow Queen of Andersen's fairy tale. She is insensitive, unfeeling, and uncaring.

Other elements from Andersen's fairy tale, whose main purpose is clearly a statement about alienation, are also carried over to Vinge's novel. Sparks, like Kay, the boy whose heart is pierced by a sliver of magic mirror, turns cold. Moon, like Gerda, the heroine of the tale, must make a difficult journey through a land of ice and snow to save Sparks with her love.

Moon is the most interesting cold symbol, for while the whiteness associated with the moon clearly links it to the image cluster and therefore implies alienation, a condition from which Moon does of course suffer, it is also the primary color of the New Moon phase of the "White Goddess," which is associated with rebirth and growth. The moon, like snow, is ambivalent. While it signifies alienation on one hand, it holds out the promise of renewal and regeneration on the other.

While the dying and revivifying vegetation archetype is not as obvious in her other stories, it is clearly present in some form. Always after passing through a "winter phase," Vinge holds out the promise of renewal with the onset of spring. It is more easily identified if one remembers that the vegetation archetype is itself a more specific statement of the life principle. It must also be remembered that while the archetype is a major device in Vinge's work, it is merely supportive of a psychological point of view that dominates her stories. Simply stated, all of us must pass through a period of alienation in order to achieve maturity and productivity that can be considered psychologically healthy. We transcend our alienation by communicating fully with one another. Because it is the most fundamental means of communicating, love is the most frequent instigator of this evolution of personality. And because love is achieved, so too is integrity, identity, independence, pride of self, creativity, productivity, and happiness.

For Vinge then, alienation is a normal developmental process, a position with which many psychologists and psychiatrists agree. David Oken writes, for instance, that turbulence and alienation are essential features of the identity crisis that characterizes alienation and further that "a placid, unruffled adolescence is a danger sign, indicating that the struggle was felt to be so fearsome that it was given up before it could be started." In this opinion, he confirms Erich Fromm's view that alienation is evolutionary. Inevitably, Vinge's major characters suffer this "trial by fire" and pass through their hellish alienation to achieve a rebirth. Like Proserpine, each figuratively and psychologically spends a period of time in the underground.

A perfect example is found in the symbolic descent made by Moon in *The Snow Queen*. Near the end of her search for Sparks, she is referred to a casino in Carbuncle run by a woman named Persipone, who turns out to be an old acquaintance, Tor Starhiker. A place for drugs, gambling, prostitution, and other sins, the casino is sketched as a symbolic hell when Tor leads Moon and BZ through "the spillover of a holo-grammic Black Gate, engulfed in flaming flotsam." The imagery is unmistakable.

Moon survives her metaphoric descent, of course, and leaves the casino not only with the means of entering Arienrhod's castle, where she saves Sparks by making love to him, but also with the location of the Old Empire's computer, which is, she discovers, located in the bedrock beneath the castle.

In making her figurative descent to hell, Moon has also made a psychological journey of vast dimension. Like the heroines and heroes of Vinge's other stories, she is back from Persipone's, a more mature and psychologically healthy person.

Notes

PAGE	QUOTE	SOURCE

1. Leigh Brackett: No Long Goodbye (Arbur)

2   "was one of our teachers"   Author's telephone interview with Bradbury, August 1981.

3   "science fiction writers care"   Ibid.

3   "a first-draft writer"   Ibid.

3   "undisputed Queen of Space Opera"   Anthony Boucher, review of *The Long Tomorrow*, *Magazine of Fantasy and Science Fiction* 10:1 (January 1956), pp. 93–94.

5   "for the modern, Marxist-oriented critic"   Author's telephone interview with Williamson, August 1981.

5   "I waited too long"   Author's interview with Bradley, March 1979.

5   "improved sharply in quality"   John Clute, "Leigh Brackett," in *The Science Fiction Encyclopedia*, Peter Nicholls, ed. (New York: Doubleday and Co., 1979), p. 85.

6   "he strongly implied"   From review of *The Best of Leigh Brackett* by Algis Budrys, *The Magazine of Fantasy and Science Fiction* 53:6 (December 1977), pp. 22–25.

6   "The tale of adventure"   Leigh Brackett, *The Best of Planet Stories No. 1* (New York: Ballantine, 1975), pp. 2–3.

9   "back when it counted"   Donald A. Wollheim in *The Universe Makers* (New York: Harper and Row, 1971), pp. 62–66.

PAGE	QUOTE	SOURCE
10	"get out and see the country"	Leigh Brackett, "All the Colors of the Rainbow," in *The Halfling and Other Stories* (New York: Ace Books, 1973), p. 146.
11	"It had rained in the valley"	Ibid., p. 143.
11	"loss of splendor"	Leigh Brackett, in *The Double Bill Symposium*, Bill Mallardi and Bill Bowers, eds. (Akron, Ohio: DB Press, 1969), p. 90.
11	a silent pause	Leigh Brackett: *The Secret of Sinharat* (New York: Ace Books, 1964), p. 94.
12	"She was tall"	*Planet Stories No. 1*, pp. 18–19.
13	"Leigh was the best"	Budrys, *The Best of Leigh Brackett*, p. 23.
13	"Thank you"	Lester del Rey's review of *The Best of Edmond Hamilton* (edited by Leigh Brackett) in *Analog* 97:8 (August 1977), p. 172.

BIBLIOGRAPHIES

Works by Leigh Brackett

The Secret of Sinharat and *People of the Talisman* (New York: Ace Books, 1964). Both feature Stark.

The Halfling and Other Stories (New York: Ace Books, 1973).

The Hounds of Skaith (New York: Ballantine, 1974).

The Coming of the Terrans (New York: Ace Books, 1976). Sequentially arranged collection of stories that bears fruitful comparison with Bradbury's *The Martian Chronicles*.

The Reavers of Skaith (New York: Ballantine, 1976).

The Starmen of Llyrdis (New York: Ballantine, 1976). Reprint of *The Starmen*, listed here because it is her first science fiction novel.

The Best of Leigh Brackett (New York: Ballantine, 1977).

The Ginger Star (New York: Ballantine, 1979).

The Sword of Rhiannon (Boston: Gregg Press, 1979).

The Long Tomorrow (New York: Ballantine, 1980).

(Dates supplied are those of the most recent publication.)

Works about Leigh Brackett

"Afterword" (by Brackett) in *The Best of Leigh Brackett*. (New York: Ballantine, 1977).

"An Interview with Leigh Brackett and Edmond Hamilton." *Science Fiction Review* 6:2 (May 1977), 6–15.

"Edmond Hamilton and Leigh Brackett." In *Speaking of Science Fiction*, Paul Walker, ed. (Oradell, New Jersey: Luna Publications, 1978).

PAGE	QUOTE	SOURCE

2. C. L. Moore's Classic SF (Mathews)

14 "I love description" — Guest of Honor Speech, Denvention II, 1981.

14 "I do think in three dimensions" — Opening remarks, introduction of the Guests of Honor, Denvention II, 1981.

15 Jirel — Pronounced Jye-*rell* by the author.

15 "Science fiction is" — C. J. Cherryh at the *C. L. Moore and Heroic Fantasy* panel, Denvention II, 1981.

15 "Through all that was Smith" and "Smith's eyes, pale and resolute" — C. L. Moore, "Shambleau," in *The Best of C. L. Moore*, Lester del Rey, ed. (New York: Ballantine Books, 1975). Original copyright 1933 by Popular Fiction Publishing Co. for *Weird Tales*.

16 "She isn't a human being any more" — C. L. Moore, "No Woman Born," in *The Best of C. L. Moore*. Original copyright 1944 by Street & Smith Publications, Inc. for *Astounding Science Fiction*.

16 "Moore's story is an important one" — Pamela Sargent, "Introduction: Women and Science Fiction," in *Women of Wonder* (New York: Vintage Books, 1975), pp. xix–xx.

17 "My brain's human" — "No Woman Born," p. 288.

17 "How much of civilization" — C. L. Moore, *Judgment Night* (New York: Dell Publishing, 1979), p. 12.

17 A fair sample of her culture: "You were the spokesman for your race, chosen fairly, typical of your kind . . ." — Ibid., p. 173.

17 "by the Hundred Emperors, I will!" — Ibid., p. 11.

18 many say finest — Among them, Marion Zimmer Bradley, quoted below from "Something More than Fantasy," in *Thrust—Science Fiction in Review* 12 (Fall 1979), p. 14. Originally printed in *Kolvir #1*, 1978.

18 "Jirel, in men's clothing" — Ibid., p. 14.

18 "In 1978, a writer" — Bradley's article was first published in 1978; "Black God's Kiss," in 1937 (actually 1934).

18 "Jirel, burning with rage" — "Something More than Fantasy," p. 14.

PAGE	QUOTE	SOURCE
18	"There is no light"	C. L. Moore, "Black God's Kiss," in *Black God's Shadow* (West Kingston, Rhode Island: Donald M. Grant, 1977), p. 53. Original copyright 1934 by Weird Tales, Inc.
19	"all the ugliness of Guillaume"	Ibid., p. 75.
19	"so just, yet so infinitely unjust"	Ibid., p. 76.
20	"Why had she"	C. L. Moore, "Jirel Meets Magic," in *Black God's Shadow*, p. 115. Original copyright 1935 by Weird Tales, Inc.
20	"Rage at life" and "her own violence"	Ibid., pp. 145–146.
20	"there is in you"	C. L. Moore, "The Dark Land," in *Black God's Shadow*, p. 163. Original copyright 1936 by Weird Tales, Inc.
20	"So I have taken you for my own"	Italics mine.
20	"I am not"	"The Dark Land," p. 177.
21	Lady Death	Nowhere is her name mentioned, but the description makes her identity obvious, especially as she lives in a Plutonian underworld of darkness and death.
21	"Let me slay"	Ibid., p. 180.
21	"the Darkness was Romne"	Ibid., p. 196.
22	"If I were a man"	*Judgment Night*, p. 10.
22	"To her mind"	*Judgment Night*, p. 14.
23	"Kleph's race"	C. L. Moore, "Vintage Season," in *The Best of C. L. Moore*, p. 362.
24	"Jirel shrugged"	"Jirel Meets Magic," p. 113.

3. Humanity Amid the Hardware (Schlobin)

26	"There are those among"	Norton, "Introduction," *Gate of Ivrel* by C. J. Cherryh (New York: DAW Books, 1976), p. 7.
27	Xenophon's *Anabasis*	John Rowe Townsend, *A Sense of Story: Essays on Contemporary Writers for Children* (Philadelphia: J. B. Lippincott, 1971), p. 145.
28	"For a long time"	Norton, *Wraiths of Time* (New York: Atheneum, 1976), p. 31.

PAGE   QUOTE   SOURCE
28   vast power structures   For a further discussion of Norton's at-
                                      titude toward power structures, see Rick
                                      Brooks, "Andre Norton: Loss of Faith,"
                                      The Dipple Chronicle 1 (November/Decem-
                                      ber 1971), 12–30; reprinted in *The Many
                                      Worlds of Andre Norton*, Roger Edwood,
                                      ed. (Radnor, Pennsylvania: Chilton, 1974),
                                      pp. 178–200.
29   "Sometimes he thought"   Norton, *Star Gate* (New York: Harcourt,
                                      Brace, 1958), p. 192.
30   "But in the name of"   Norton, *Octagon Magic* (Cleveland: World,
                                      1967), p. 106.
30   "Yes, I am anti-machine."   Norton as quoted by Rick Brooks, in *The
                                      Dipple Chronicle*, p. 22; in *The Many Worlds
                                      of Andre Norton*, p. 191.
30   "Miss Norton handles"   Townsend, *A Sense of Story*, p. 148.
31   *Merlin's Mirror*   Andre Norton (New York: DAW Books,
                                      1975). See p. 91 for an example of Merlin
                                      and the raven.
31   *Star Guard*   (New York: Harcourt, Brace, 1955). See
                                      especially p. 151.

BIBLIOGRAPHIES

Selected Works by Andre Norton

Star Man's Son 2250 A.D. (New York: Harcourt, Brace, 1952).
Star Guard (New York: Harcourt, Brace, 1955).
Star Gate (New York: Harcourt, Brace, 1958).
The Beast Master (New York: Harcourt, Brace, 1959).
Eye of the Monster (New York: Harcourt, Brace, 1959).
Steel Magic (Cleveland: World, 1965). Later titled *Grey Magic* (1967).
Octagon Magic (Cleveland: World, 1967).
Merlin's Mirror (New York: DAW Books, 1975).
Iron Butterflies (New York: Fawcett Crest, 1980).
Lore of the Witch World (New York: DAW Books, 1980).
Voorloper (New York: Ace Books, 1980).
Gryphon in Glory (New York: Atheneum, 1981).
Horn Crown (New York: DAW Books, 1981).
Ten Mile Treasure (New York: Pocket/Archway, 1981).

Related Works

Beeler, Thomas T. "Introduction." In *The Time Traders* by Andre Norton
    (Boston: Gregg, 1978).

PAGE   QUOTE   SOURCE

Brooks, Rick. "Andre Norton: Loss of Faith." *The Dipple Chronicle* 1 (November/ December 1971), 12–30; reprinted in *The Many Worlds of Andre Norton*, Roger Elwood, ed. (Radnor, Pennsylvania, Chilton, 1974), 178–200. Later title: *The Book of Andre Norton* (New York: DAW Books, 1975).

Fisher, Margery. "Writers for Children: 8. Andre Norton." *The School Librarian* 15 (July 1967), 141–44.

Fraser, Brian. "Putting the Past into the Future. Interview with Andre Norton." *Fantastic Science Fiction* (October 1980), 4–9.

Hodgson, William Hope. *The Nightland: A Love Tale* (New York: Ballantine, 1972).

Lethbridge, T. C. *ESP: Beyond Time and Distance* (London: Scientific Book Club, 1965).

McGhan, Barry. "Andre Norton: Why Has She Been Neglected?" *Riverside Quarterly* 4 (January 1970), 128–31.

Miesel, Sandra. "Introduction." In *Sargasso of Space* by Andre Norton (Boston: Gregg, 1978).

Russ, Gary Alan. "*Algol* Profile: Andre Norton." *Algol* 14 (Summer/Fall 1977), 15–17.

Schlobin, Roger C. *Andre Norton: A Primary and Secondary Bibliography* (Boston: G. K. Hall, 1980).

Townsend, John Rowe. "Andre Norton." In *A Sense of Story: Essays on Contemporary Writers for Children* (Philadelphia: J. B. Lippincott, 1971), 143–53.

Weinkauf, Mary S. "The Indian in Science Fiction." *Extrapolation* 20 (1979), 308–320.

Yoke, Carl B. *Roger Zelazny and Andre Norton: Proponents of Individualism* (Columbus: The State Library of Ohio, 1979).

4. C. J. Cherryh and Tomorrow's New Sex Roles (Brizzi)

PAGE	QUOTE	SOURCE
32	epic heroines	For a partial list of SF works with heroines, see George Fergus, "A Checklist of SF Novels with Female Protagonists," *Extrapolation* 18:1 (December 1976), pp. 20–27.
41	"the stone or rock"	Matt. 16:18.
42	"sang a hymn"	Ibid., 26:30.
42	"kept his hands"	C. J. Cherryh, *The Faded Sun: Shon'jir* (New York: DAW Books, 1979), Ch. 5.
42	"as Christ was"	Matt. 4:1–11.
42	"The foxes have"	Ibid., 8:20.
43	"publicans and sinners"	Ibid., 9:10.
43	"I am the foretold"	C. J. Cherryh, *The Faded Sun: Kutath* (New York: DAW Books, 1980), Ch. 11.

PAGE	QUOTE	SOURCE
44	"perhaps qhalish"	C. J. Cherryh, *Fires of Azeroth* (New York: DAW Books, 1979), Ch. 14.
46	" 'Never,' she said"	Ibid., Ch. 17.

5. Toward New Sexual Identities (Frisch)

48	"For those who"	James Tiptree, Jr., "Lirios: A Tale of the Quintana Roo," in *Isaac Asimov's Science Fiction Magazine* 5:10 (Sept. 28, 1981), p. 167.
48	"interview . . . in Locus"	ed. Charles Brown, January 1977.
49	"Houston, Houston"	"Houston, Houston, Do You Read?" in *Aurora: Beyond Equality*, Susan Anderson and Vonda McIntyre, eds. (New York: Fawcett, 1976).
50	"save society"	"Houston," in *Nebula Winners Twelve*, Gordon R. Dickson, ed. (New York: Harper & Row, 1978), p. 235.
50	"the primordial Big Man"	"A Momentary Taste of Being," in *The New Atlantis*, Robert Silverberg, ed. (New York: Hawthorn Books, 1975), p. 133.
50	"The Psychologist"	"The Psychologist Who Wouldn't Do Awful Things to Rats," in *New Dimensions 6*, Robert Silverberg, ed. (New York: Ballantine, 1976).
51	"opossums"	"The Women Men Don't See," *Magazine of Fantasy and Science Fiction* 57:4 (October 1979), p. 142. The story was first published in *F&SF* in December 1973.
51	"Men live to struggle"	"The Women," p. 142.
51	"The Screwfly Solution"	"The Screwfly Solution" was first published under the pseudonym of Raccoona Sheldon in *1978 Annual World's Best Science Fiction*, Donald Wollheim, ed. (New York: DAW Books, 1978).
51	"Her Smoke"	"Her Smoke Rose Up Forever," in *Final Stage*, Edward C. Ferman and Barry N. Malzberg, eds. (New York: Charterhouse, 1974).
52	"haploid condition"	Lowri Pei, "Poor Singletons: Definitions of Humanity in the Stories of James Tiptree, Jr.," in *Science Fiction Studies* 6:3

PAGE	QUOTE	SOURCE
		(November 1979), pp. 271–280. Uses Tiptree's 1969 short story entitled "Your Haploid Heart" as a basis for studying the importance of individuality in her works.
52	"She Waits"	"She Waits for All Men Born," in *Future Power*, Jack Dann and Gardner R. Dozois, eds. (New York: Random House, 1976), p. 73.
52	"the last human"	Ibid. p. 73.
53	"life-hungry succubus"	"Lirios," pp. 166–167.
54	*Up the Walls*	*Up the Walls of the World* (New York: Berkley, 1978).
54	"I love"	Ibid., p. 8.
55	"What else"	*Up the Walls*, p. 23.
56	"intolerable stress" and "great contradiction"	*Up the Walls*, p. 245.
56	"We emerge"	"The Women," p. 131.
57	"Love Is the Plan"	"Love Is the Plan, the Plan is Death," in *The Alien Condition*, Stephen Goldin, ed. (New York: Ballantine, 1973).
57	"The Milk"	"The Milk of Paradise," in *Again, Dangerous Visions*, Harlan Ellison, ed. (New York: New American Library, 1972).
57	"Her mind"	*Up the Walls*, p. 195.
58	"world's biggest"	"The Women," p. 127.
58	"soaked in slime"	"The Women," p. 132.
58	"dense dying with life"	*Up the Walls*, p. 38.
58	"She is Tivonel"	*Up the Walls*, pp. 11–12.
58	"Doctor Daniel Dann"	*Up the Walls*, p. 18.
58	"I must follow"	*Up the Walls*, pp. 246–248.

6. Holding Fast to Feminism (Barr)

PAGE	QUOTE	SOURCE
60	"a story of society"	Suzy McKee Charnas, "A Woman Appeared," in *Future Females: A Critical Analogy*, Marleen S. Barr, ed. (Bowling Green, Ohio: Bowling Green University Popular Press, 1981), p. 104.
60	"To begin with"	"A Woman Appeared," p. 426.
61	"possibly the outstanding"	Charles N. Brown, "The Science Fiction Year," in *The Best Science Fiction of the Year* (New York: Pocket Books, 1981), p. 426.

PAGE	QUOTE	SOURCE
61	"that whole traditional"	Victoria Schochet and John Silbersack eds., "Elizabeth A. Lynn: An Interview" in *The Berkley Showcase* (New York: Berkley, 1981), pp. 193–94.
62	"Ah—what about"	Suzy McKee Charnas, *Vampire* (New York: Simon and Schuster, 1980), p. 141.
62	"one of the best realized"	George R. R. Martin, *New Voices III* (New York: Berkley 1980), p. 79.
63	"My grandfather"	*Vampire*, p. 18.
63	"like scarcely more"	*Vampire*, p. 22.
63	"from lady of leisure"	*Vampire*, p. 32.
63	"vaccuming the"	*Vampire*, p. 32.
63	"If Weyland could"	*Vampire*, p. 51.
63	"devastating stroke"	*Vampire*, p. 282.
64	"Katje De Groot the huntress"	*Vampire*, p. 269.
64	"the heroine is, as a rule"	H. R. Steeves, "Gothic Romance," in *Colliers Encylopedia* (New York: Macmillan, 1980), Vol. 11.
65	"This is the hour"	*Vampire*, p. 206.
66	"Isn't it extremely unprofessional"	*Vampire*, p. 169.
66	"an ambitious woman"	*Vampire*, p. 169.
66	"If her friends"	*Vampire*, p. 124.
66	"without need, without hunger"	*Vampire*, p. 210.
66	"I think what shocks them"	*Vampire*, p. 215.
67	"How to distinguish"	*Vampire*, p. 221.
67	"Reese's creatures"	*Vampire*, p. 282.
68	"Weyland's bloodied hand"	*Vampire*, p. 280.
68	"Maybe it wouldn't be too far"	*Vampire*, p. 200.
68	"You're right about him"	*Vampire*, p. 203.
68	"like watching"	*Vampire*, p. 200.
68	"Where did it come from"	*Vampire*, p. 223.
69	"Scarpia was . . ."	*Vampire*, p. 210.
69	"You're planning some politely"	*Vampire*, p. 234.
69	"Female graduate students"	*Vampire*, p. 253.
69	"scholarship [which] was"	*Vampire*, p. 246.
69	"hustled along trundling"	*Vampire*, p. 231.
69	"hunger"	*Vampire*, p. 235.
69	". . . young Ph.D's"	*Vampire*, p. 127.

PAGE	QUOTE	SOURCE
70	"that humans are also animals"	*Vampire*, p. 151.
70	"Complete replacement"	*Vampire*, p. 243.
70	". . . the robot as commodity"	Alessandro Portelli, "The Three Laws of Robotics," in *Science Fiction Studies #21* (July 1980), p. 154.
71	"kicking our bodies"	*Vampire*, p. 45.
71	"He could not hunt"	*Vampire*, p. 284.
71	"Now he knew with bitter"	*Vampire*, p. 284.
71	"He had begun to take"	*Vampire*, p. 283.
72	"Not cattle these"	*Vampire*, p. 283.
72	"He was in his own way"	*Vampire*, p. 270.

7. Marion Zimmer Bradley's Ethic of Freedom (Shwartz)

75	"Ha! The Domains live"	Marion Zimmer Bradley, *The Shattered Chain* (New York: DAW Books, 1976, reprinted 1977), pp. 25–26.
75	"early freed herself"	Ibid., p. 26. Italics supplied.
75	"who truly chose" and "will pay the price"	Ibid., p. 26. Italics supplied.
75	"There is always an alternative"	Ibid., p. 26.
76	"By Dry-Town custom"	Ibid., pp. 16–17.
76	"If they wish to"	Ibid., p. 17.
76	"I don't know what"	Ibid., p. 82.
78	"had paid the Keeper's price"	Ibid., p. 58.
78	"It is her right"	Ibid., p. 75.
78	"He is a male"	Ibid., p. 76.
79	"Blood-feud and revenge"	Ibid., p. 77.
79	"Am I only"	Ibid., p. 81.
79	"Now that I know"	Ibid., p. 83.
80	"there are those"	Ibid., p. 84.
80	"her old life"	Ibid., p. 90.
82	"If I fail"	Ibid., p. 5.
82	"I didn't mind"	Ibid., p. 158.
82	"I wanted so"	Ibid., p. 159.
83	"giving herself"	Ibid., p. 229.
83	"rape made lawful"	Ibid., p. 243.

PAGE	QUOTE	SOURCE
84	"You damnable Amazon bitches"	Ibid., p. 251.
84	"A woman not free"	Ibid., p. 272.
85	"a great door"	Ibid., p. 284.
86	"he who had once sworn"	Marion Zimmer Bradley, *Heritage of Hastur* (New York: DAW Books, 1976, reprinted 1977), p. 164.
87	"If you have any flaw"	Ibid., p. 211.
87	"Not his wish"	Ibid., p. 376.
87	"And then"	Ibid., p. 381.
88	"I did not say"	Ibid., p. 273.

BIBLIOGRAPHIES

Works by Marion Zimmer Bradley

The Planet Savers (New York: Ace Books, 1962, reprinted 1976). (Includes "The Waterfall")

The Sword of Aldones (New York: Ace Books, 1962, reprinted 1976).

The Bloody Sun (New York: Ace Books, 1964, reprinted 1975; rewritten and enlarged, 1979). (Includes "To Keep the Oath.")

Star of Danger (New York: Ace Books, 1966, reprinted 1975).

Winds of Darkover (New York: Ace Books, 1970, reprinted 1977).

The World Wreckers (New York: Ace Books, 1971, reprinted 1977).

Darkover Landfall (New York: Ace Books, 1972, reprinted 1977).

The Spell Sword (New York: DAW Books, 1972, reprinted 1975).

Heritage of Hastur (New York: DAW Books, 1976, reprinted 1977) (Written with Lew Alton and Regis Hastur.)

The Shattered Chain (New York: DAW Books, 1976, reprinted 1977).

Forbidden Tower (New York: DAW Books, 1977).

Stormqueen (New York: DAW Books, 1978).

Two to Conquer (New York: DAW Books, 1980).

The Keeper's Price (New York: DAW Books, 1980) (Anthology of Bradley's stories and professional published fan fiction. Includes "Blood Will Tell.") (Second anthology to be published New York: DAW Books, 1982.)

Sharra's Exile (To be published. New York: DAW Books.)

Related Works

Lynn, Elizabeth. *The Dancers of Arun* (New York: Dell Publishing, 1977).

Russ, Joanna. *We Who Are About To* (New York: Berkley-Putnam, 1979).

———. "When It Changed," in *Again, Dangerous Visions*, Harlan Ellison, ed. (New York: Doubleday and Co., 1972).

Sheldon, Alice [James Tiptree, Jr.]. "The Women Men Don't See," in *Warm Worlds and Otherwise* (New York: Ballantine, 1975).

8. Sex, Satire, and Feminism (Chapman)

89	The science fiction novels	The idea of "formula" adventure stories is widespread now, but perhaps best defined in John G. Cawelti, *Adventure, Mystery, and Romance* (Chicago: University of Chicago Press, 1976).
91	"Curiosity . . . is only useful"	S. H. Elgin, *At the Seventh Level* (New York: Daw Books, 1972), p. 71. Subsequent quotations are to this edition.
92	Elgin's Missouri childhood	One of the most detailed biographical sketches on Elgin appears in a publisher's note inside the front page of *Furthest* (New York: Ace Books, 1971). (Further references to *Furthest* pertain to this edition.)
95	"He had time"	*Furthest*, p. 93.
95	"possibilities of telepathy"	Telepathy is a "wild talent" that figures in numerous science fiction novels before Elgin, notably *Slan* (1941) by A. E. Van Vogt and *The Demolished Man* by Alfred Bester (1952). Although both of these authors advanced the cause of the telepathic novel, they did not explore the sexual possibilities of telepathy very thoroughly. Bester does permit his characters some "off-color" thoughts. I may have overlooked or been unaware of some sixties novels that explored the sexual possibilities of telepathy, however.
97	John Norman	John Norman's Gor series, commencing with *Tarnsman of Gor* in the early sixties began as an imitation of Edgar Rice Burroughs's John Carter swashbucklers. By the late sixties, the series had become the definitive expression of male chauvinism in science fiction, with women enslaved or in bondage throughout the novels.
97	"For the Love of Grace"	"For the Love of Grace" was first published in 1970 as a magazine story as "For the Sake of Grace" in *Fantasy and Science Fiction*; it was reprinted in the anthology *World's Best Science Fiction: 1970* (New York: Ace Books, 1970).

PAGE	QUOTE	SOURCE

97 "There can be no law"   *At the Seventh Level*, p. 101.

98 "I'm just trying"   *At the Seventh Level*, p. 125.

100 all the famous   S. H. Elgin, *Star-Anchored, Star-Angered* (Garden City, New York: Doubleday & Co., 1979), p. 60. Subsequent references are to this edition.

100 "First principle"   *Star-Anchored, Star-Angered*, p. 63.

100 authentic Christ-figure   I mean by "Christ-figure" an archetypal messianic figure preaching love and forgiveness, crucified and martyred.

100 numinosity   A good discussion of numinosity is found in W. T. Stace, *Mysticism and Philosophy* (Philadelphia & New York: J. B. Lippincott, 1960), pp. 292–294.

101 "roots for Elgin"   According to the notes on the jackets of the Doubleday novels, Elgin has moved to the King's River country near Huntsville, Arkansas, a remote and not very much developed area of the Ozarks. *Star-Anchored, Star-Angered* contains some strong satire on academic life, suggesting a certain disenchantment. The two volumes of the Ozark Fantasy Trilogy published this year indicate that the settlers of the planet Ozark were fleeing the evils of contemporary "civilized" life—crime, pollution, corrupt politics, a centralized bureaucracy, and a general atmosphere of mendacity. If Elgin is disenchanted by such ills, many share her feelings.

102 She realizes that satire   S. H. Elgin, *The Gentle Art of Verbal Self-Defense* (Englewood Cliffs, New Jersey: Prentice-Hall, 1980) is an impressive attempt to apply linguistic theory to the psychology of interpersonal relationships. Although strongly feminist in its point of view, the book generally tends to treat direct confrontation as a linguistic strategy of limited usefulness.

9. From Alienation to Personal Triumph (Yoke)

103 "But she wore"   Joan D. Vinge, *The Snow Queen* (New York: The Dial Press, 1980), p. 458.

PAGE	QUOTE	SOURCE
105	extreme self-alienation	Frank Johnson, "Psychological Alienation: Isolation and Self-Estrangement," in *Alienation: Concept, Term, and Meanings*, Frank Johnson, ed. (New York: Seminar Press, 1973), p. 54.
105	"Legacy"	"Legacy" is the extended version of "Media Man," which was originally published in *Analog* (October 1976).
105	"is the inextricable"	Blanche H. Gelfant, "The Imagery of Estrangement: Alienation in Modern American Fiction," in *Alienation*, p. 295.
105	While the characteristics	Edward F. Abood, *Underground Man* (San Francisco: Chandler and Sharp, 1973), p. 2.
105	Regardless of the causes	Erich Fromm, *The Sane Society* (Greenwich, Connecticut: Fawcett Publications, 1955), p. 23.
106	Since the term	Walter Kaufmann, "Introduction," *Alienation*, by Richard Schacht (New York: Doubleday and Company, 1970), p. xx.
106	"The facts to which"	Guyton B. Hammond, *Man in Estrangement* (Nashville, Tennessee: Vanderbilt University Press, 1965), pp. 11–12.
106	In describing the "Underground Man"	*Underground Man*, p. 2.
107	The latter group	"The Imagery of Estrangement," p. 307.
107	Abood confirms	*Underground Man*, pp. 7–9.
107	While accepting	*Man in Estrangement*, p. 119.
107	"Human nature" and "Transcendence"	*Man in Estrangement*, p. 122.
108	"transmuted into" and "pays the price"	Steven G. Spruill, Afterword to "Legacy" by Joan Vinge in *Binary Star #4* (New York: Dell Publishing, 1980), p. 143.
108	"She burns"	Afterword to "legacy", p. 144.
108	"those crazy bastards"	Joan D. Vinge, "Legacy," in *Binary Star #4* (New York: Dell Publishing, 1980), p. 115.
109	"Get the hell"	"Legacy," p. 115.
109	"It will be lonely"	"Legacy," p. 61.
109	"Yes, yes, yes"	"Legacy," p. 61.

PAGE	QUOTE	SOURCE
109	He has been hounded	Joan D. Vinge, "The Crystal Ship," in *Eyes of Amber and Other Stories* (New York: The New American Library, 1979), p. 181. (Originally published in *The Crystal Ship*, Robert Silverberg, ed., 1976.)
110	"She remembered the sight"	"The Crystal Ship," p. 154.
110	"But even knowing"	"The Crystal Ship," p. 181.
111	"the staid ritual life"	Joan D. Vinge, "Phoenix in the Ashes," in *Millennial Women*, Virginia Kidd, ed. (New York: Dell Publishing Company, 1979), p. 105. (Originally published in hardcover by Delacorte Press, 1978.)
111	"There's little more"	"Phoenix in the Ashes," p. 92.
111	"I use you"	"Phoenix in the Ashes," p. 83.
112	"He was gone"	Joan D. Vinge, *The Outcasts of Heaven Belt* (New York: The New American Library, 1978), p. 22.
113	She finds the system	*Outcasts*, p. 63.
113	"She cursed the Demarchy"	*Outcasts*, p. 108.
114	"a man with no family"	*Outcasts*, p. 113.
114	"The immensity of isolation"	*Outcasts*, p. 143.
114	"to live with a defect"	*Sane Society*, p. 24.
114	"She looked away again"	Joan D. Vinge, "Eyes of Amber," in *Eyes of Amber and Other Stories*, p. 27.
115	She is successful	*Sane Society*, p. 23.
115	From this point of view	Donald Oken, "Alienation and Identity: Some Comments on Adolescence, the Counterculture, and Contemporary Adaptations," in *Alienation*, p. 86.
115	"She lost track"	*Snow Queen*, p. 329.
118	"I am not what I was"	Joan D. Vinge, "Mother and Child," in *Fireship* (New York: Dell Publishing, 1978), pp. 182–183. (Originally published in *Orbit 16*, Damon Knight, ed. 1975.)
118	"The Wheel of Change"	"Eyes of Amber," p. 82.
119	The relationship among	Robert Frazier, "Interview: Joan Vinge," *Thrust* 16 (Fall 1980), p. 8.

PAGE	QUOTE	SOURCE
120	"No . . . I don't need one"	*Snow Queen*, p. 491.
121	"Afterword"	"The Crystal Ship," p. 201.
123	In those myths	Jessie L. Weston, *From Ritual to Romance* (Garden City, New York: Anchor Books, 1957), p. 21. (Originally published by Cambridge University Press, 1920.)
124	In a more general sense	*From Ritual to Romance*, p. 38.
124	The Greek myth of Proserpine . . .	*Bullfinch's Mythology* (New York: Dell Publishing, 1959), pp. 51–55.
124	While several other symbols	Frazier, "Interview: Joan Vinge," p. 8.
124	She is a goddess of the moon	Robert Graves, *The White Goddess: A Historical Grammar of Poetic Myth* (Farrar, Straus and Cudahy, 1948), p. 52.
124	"the creatress and destructress"	*White Goddess*, p. 320.
124	For each aspect of the White Goddess	*White Goddess*, p. 76.
125	"black, screaming hag"	*White Goddess*, p.117.
125	Cerridwen, the Old Moon aspect	*White Goddess*, p. 76.
125	To be under her spell	Graves, *White Goddess*, p. 77.
126	"had only two alternatives"	Vinge, *Outcasts*, p. 10.
126	"that the only true"	"Phoenix in the Ashes," p. 92.
127	"Amanda has blossomed"	"Phoenix in the Ashes," p. 116.
127	This is a side effect	*The Snow Queen*, p. 396.
127	"snow-water dashed"	"Mother and Child," p. 109.
129	"an ethereal, pale sort"	"Interview: Joan Vinge," p. 8.
130	"a placid, unruffled adolescence"	Oken, *Alienation*, p. 90.
130	"the spillover of a hologrammic Black Gate"	*The Snow Queen*, p. 389.

About the Editor

TOM STAICAR is book review columnist for *Amazing Stories* and is the Science Fiction Book Selector for the University of Michigan's Hatcher Graduate Library. He has written articles and reviews published in *Fantastic Stories, Writer's Digest, Science Fiction Review*, and other magazines. Staicar is a member of the Science Fiction Research Association and the SF Oral History Association.

About the Contributors

ROSEMARIE ARBUR compiled the G. K. Hall bibliography *Leigh Brackett, Marion Zimmer Bradley, Anne McCaffrey: A Reference Guide* and has contributed more than forty articles to journals of various types. She currently teaches literature and other subjects at Lehigh University in Bethlehem, Pennsylvania.

MARLEEN BARR is an Assistant Professor of English at Virginia Polytechnic Institute and State University. She edited *Future Females: A Critical Anthology* (Bowling Green, 1981) and wrote the article on Deborah Norris Logan in *American Women Writers*, Volume 3 (Ungar, 1981).

MARY T. BRIZZI has reviewed books for *Choice* and has published a number of poems. She is Associate Professor of English at Kent State University's Trumbull Campus. Her *Reader's Guide to Philip José Farmer* (Starmont) was published in 1979.

EDGAR L. CHAPMAN wrote the essay on one of Philip K. Dick's novels for Magill's *Salem Survey of Science Fiction* (Salem, 1979) and has prepared a guide to Philip José Farmer's works forthcoming from Borgo Press.

ADAM J. FRISCH has a Ph.D. in English Literature from the University of Texas at Austin. He contributed two essays in the Greenwood Press series of SF studies.

PATRICIA MATHEWS lives in Albuquerque, N. M., and has been active in SF fandom, participating in the Marion Zimmer Bradley fan group The Friends of Darkover. Bradley described her as "perhaps the finest single writing talent" discovered by that group. She selected three of Mathews's short stories for publication in *The Keeper's Price* (DAW Books, 1979) and *Swords of Chaos* (DAW Books, 1982).

ROGER C. SCHLOBIN is a highly respected SF scholar. Author of such works as *The Literature of Fantasy: A Comprehensive Annotated Bibliography* (Garland, 1979) and series editor for the Starmont Reader's Guide series and the Garland Fantasy Classics collection, Schlobin is the official bibliographer for Andre Norton.

SUSAN M. SHWARTZ has a Ph.D. in Medieval Literature from Harvard University. She has published articles in *Omni* and *Fantasy Newsletter* and short stories in *Analog*, and was one of the winners of the *Village Voice* SF writing contest in 1981. Marion Zimmer Bradley's anthology *The Keeper's Price* (DAW Books, 1979) includes one of her stories.

CARL YOKE is Assistant to the Vice President at Kent State University and has published many articles about SF. He was formerly associate editor of the SF journal *Extrapolation*. Starmont published his *Readers' Guide to Roger Zelazny* in 1979.